WEAVING WORDS

- MARJORIE BANKS

- MARIA P FRINO

- CONCHITA GARSANTIAGO

- JOANNA MAKRIS

- IRINA GLADUSHCHENKO

- ADELAIDE HUNTER

- MARIA ISSARIS

- MAREE WALK

WOMEN ABOUT WOMEN

Copyright

© Women About Women, 2022. All rights reserved.

No part of this book may be reproduced in any form or by any electronic or mechanical means, including information storage and retrieval systems, without written permission from the author, except for the use of brief quotations in a book review.

First published in 2022. The moral rights of the authors have been asserted. All rights reserved. Except as permitted under the Australian Copyright Act 1968 (for example, a fair dealing for the purposes of study, research, criticism or review), no part of this book may be reproduced, stored in a retrieval system, communicated or transmitted in any form or by any means without prior written permission. This is a work of fiction.

Cover Design: Liam Prendergast - @liamprendesigns

Audio book production - Maria Issaris, www.audiobooksradio.com.au

All inquiries to – WAWanthology@gmail.com

❀ Created with Vellum

FOREWORD

Weaving Words Anthology
Women About Women
Cass Moriarty

When I was invited to write a foreword for this anthology, Weaving Words, and given some insight into its creation and development, I immediately appreciated the concept and the project, and especially the passion of the women involved. The premise is simple: thirteen short stories of fiction from eight emerging women writers, but the finished result is more than the sum of its parts. This anthology is a wonderful example of women lifting up other women, of writers supporting writers, of a community coming together to fulfil ambitions and dreams.

This group of writers originally met online and formed a writing group – Women About Women – in the midst of Covid, with the objectives to provide advice, support and encouragement to each other in their writing, and to join together to spark inspiration and ideas. They set a goal of producing an anthology for International Women's Day 2022. Their mission statement is: *'To give all women the opportunity to express their imagination through writing and to continue honing their writing skills.'* After reading the stories contained in this anthology, I believe they have reached their goal, and I suspect the publication of Weaving Words will inspire them to continue to search for ideas, to develop new skills and to improve their creative writing practice.

The first story, **A Slice of Moon**, by Maria Issaris, is the perfect choice to open this collection. With a distinct voice, rich characters and grim humour, this story pulls the reader directly into the narrative and immerses us in a family's pain.

Author Conchita GarSantiago has contributed two stories. The first, **Aunty Tessa**, explores friendship and is set in Spain; it has a strong feeling of historical auto-fiction or perhaps informed by memoir. Her second tale, **The Rings**, is a layered examination of family secrets, abuse and shame, with a menacing sense of creeping tension and suspense.

The Brothers Karamazov, by Maree Walk, takes us back to 1978 and examines relationships and the heady days of youthful travelling abroad, the freedom of adventure and the pain of lost love.

Maria P. Frino has also contributed two stories, each quite different. **Dahlia's Garden** is a fascinating mix of science, development and climate change issues, combined with a very personal story of the love of gardening, and the long tail of grief and how best to memorialise those lost. Her second story, **The White Shoe**, is a mysterious tale of memories, sleep disorders and dreams, set in three different times, with the ties between past and present only becoming obvious towards the conclusion.

Writer Joanna Makris' two contributions each give teasing and light-hearted glimpses into the lives of others, especially her story **The Neurotic Nomad**, in which a house-sitter slips into other people's skins as she moves from home to home. Makris' short story **Confessions** is full of misunderstandings and mystery as the provenance of a family heirloom comes into question.

The two stories written by Adelaide Hunter both deal with ghosts and tragedies. **The Dig** examines an ancient archaeological dig site, and **Enchantment** explores the grief and loss of loved ones through the lens of an unsettling and sinister mysticism.

Irina Gladushchenko's first story, **The Invisible Cloud**, explores family, love, regret and gratefulness. Her second contribution, **Leilani's Magick,** is an esoteric tale of mysticism rooted in a deep appreciation of the natural world.

Author Marjorie Banks' cosy crime story about a potential poisoning is a refreshing, contemporary inclusion. **June's Casseroles** is deliciously cheeky and fun.

The collective themes of this anthology include family, memories, history, relationship dynamics, foreign lands, art, lost opportunities and missed chances, grief and loss and the search for self-identity. About finding your place in the world. About interactions with others and the emotions that result. Most if not all of the stories gravitate towards some of these issues. But more importantly, each story is told with a passion that shines through with the author's words.

Weaving Words is an ambitious anthology by a group of diverse women authors who use writing to find themselves and to search for meaning and independence. I'm always so heartened to find collections published by like-minded writers who develop strength, power and confidence through banding together and presenting their work collectively. I encourage each of these women to continue on their writing journeys through building important skills and offering each other the support and encouragement to pursue further literary goals.

Maria Issaris stopped writing reports and policies a few years back, and started writing other stuff. She wrote a first novel, started a second, co-edited an Anthology with the Sydney School of Arts, published a short story in the inaugural Authora Australis literary magazine, and developed a radio program on new writers which was short-listed as Best New Program 2020. She is now working in radio and publishing, organises writers groups, and has started an audiobook production business to ensure stories get told in every possible way.

A Slice of Moon

Maria Issaris

When they moved him to Goulburn, Daphne decided to visit, arriving at my place with a dozen suitcases, and god knows how she got those on the plane all the way across the Atlantic without paying a small fortune in excess baggage.

We travelled there together, a town made of sandstone of such a colour that the whole town lit up golden red for those few moments of sunset when we arrived, as if it were breathing in those last moments of sun. We needed to stay overnight to register for the visit the next morning. We liked sleeping together; Daphne would kick and make sharp movements and I would push at her to keep still, and we could forget for a moment that we were grown-ups and slip back into being two girls sharing a bed at home – nothing happening in the outside world mattering more than gaining that extra inch of bed on your side, nestling down into the most comfortable position possible and winning the fight for sleep by telling your sister to shut up and stop talking.

We set out for the jail in our hire car – a model that was smarter than the grade of car I had ordered online because Daphne had fronted up to the car rental people looking like a perturbed celebrity, frowning in disdain at the little Micra we had been assigned.

'You don't have anything else?' she had asked, pushing her vintage Chanel tote bag out of the way, turning to look over the field of cars, peering out through her squared off Prada sunglasses.

We drove off eventually in a little Audi and started to cruise around, me at the wheel and Daphne navigating, and getting lost. Goulburn has a flatland geography, and somehow the famously large sandstone prison did not stick out above any of the other buildings - a muddle of history, practicality, a buffering of time.

'Okay. Now how do we ask for directions without mentioning the word jail?' I muttered as we parked momentarily to get our bearings. We studied the map and found some adjacent landmarks. Ah yes, we could see a tennis court marked opposite the jail on the map. Perfect.

By now we were in the back streets, which had become alarmingly rural. Fields stretched out behind rickety weather-beaten fences – fields of yellow stubble that could have been wheat, could have been hay.

We asked someone on the street, a middle-aged guy trudging his way on the tussocky footpaths. Maybe he was middle-aged; he had that type of dusty coloured hair that makes a man age-indeterminate, a bleached-out look Anglo-derived people get when they grow up in this southern sun. Daphne and I would often joke that Anglos simply did not belong in this country, that their skin could not tolerate it.

Daphne hailed him with, 'Oh, excuse me, excuse me.' She had put on one of those high-pitched, little-girl voices that she thinks comes across as sweet. I noticed that men liked it. He stopped and turned. This guy had spent a lot of time outdoors and his blue eyes shot sharp out of his creased face.

'Would you happen to know how we can get to the tennis courts, please?' she asked, flicking her hair and smiling. *Count yourself lucky I am giving you my attention, I could hear her thinking.*

The man crossed his arms, and cocked his head to one side.

'Tennis courts,' he said mulling it over in his mouth. 'I can't recall any tennis courts this side of town ... tennis courts ...'

'Oh, they're on the map, but if you don't know, that's fine ...' she said, making to close the map up, but he stretched his hand to grab at it.

'Let's see the map, then,' he said as Daphne submitted to his inward thrusting hands, rearing back into her leather seat, but keeping a tight hold on one corner. He looked at us more closely, staring at our clothes, peering into the car.

I smiled at him, one of those overly nice 'don't fuck with me smiles' you learn to use in the country. The man gave a small 'hmph' in response and studied the map.

'Oh, those ...', he said, jabbing his blunt brown finger in the vicinity of the courts we had marked with a pen. 'Those courts have been closed for years, yeeeears.' He dragged out the word to emphasise the notion of time, shaking his head.

Daphne and I started to fidget, and I began to mumble something about getting going. He wouldn't have it, and tugged at the map, Daphne tugging on her end, so the map was now stretched halfway out the car window.

'But if you head towards the jail,' he said, 'you will see where they once were.'

'Jail?' asked Daphne as if it were a word that confused her.

'Yeah, the jail ...' he drawled. 'You can't miss it once you get up close, it's ...'. He launched into a maze of directions. '... and then if you veer to the left you will find yourselves right outside the jail ... and the closed tennis courts ... they're right across the road.' We looked intently at the map as if studying it. 'From the jail,' he added. Just for fun, I was guessing.

He waved us goodbye as I lurched the car forward. 'Do you

remember what he said?' I asked Daphne as I looked into the rear-view mirror only to see him, arms folded, watching us leave.

'No, no, not a thing. I was ...' she shook her head as if doing so would free her of her thoughts and sort out her curls at the same time. I wondered if she knew how often she did this. 'Let's just go straight there and get this over with.'

I peered sideways. Daphne had turned away to look out the window, her arms crossed, looking cranky and sullen. I wanted to poke her in the ribs like we used to when we were kids. I did. She hit me back, and soon we were tangled in slaps, bursting into laughter, her strange hiccuppy giggle making me laugh more, and then I had to brake suddenly at a stop light, making us fall forward sharp onto our seatbelts, which sobered us up.

'Just concentrate on the road, will you?' she said authoritatively, and started tidying herself up, checking her perfectly made-up face – which was so perfectly made-up, it looked completely natural, but better – and extracting from her soft leather bag a lipstick gloss, applying it in the car-shade mirror swiftly. The lip gloss was like no earthly colour; blood and pearls and gold mixed together. On her lips it looked like something delicious had melted there.

Daphne sighed, and after inspecting my face, which her look told me was completely unsatisfactory to her eye, begrudgingly handed the gloss to me.

'Here,' she said impatiently , 'just put this on when we get there. You need it.' And she could not help adding, 'But only a smear. It's my limited edition Paloma Picasso gloss. Very rare.' She followed this piece of information with, 'And look in the mirror when you do it, would you? None of this, this and this ...' she mimed exaggerated scrawling hand movements over her face to demonstrate my ineptitude at lipstick application. I retaliated with a cynical sneer but grabbed the gloss before she changed her mind.

'And I'm hungry,' she added. Daphne was always hungry. God knows how she kept so thin. It was like sitting next to a tight-strung harp.

~

The jail finally reared out of the landscape like the bones of some ancient beast beached and bleached, dark crevices in the moulded sandstone.

Daphne stepped out of the car, taking her time, arranging her accessories; watch laced with simple bracelets, bag fitting the geometry of her clothing, while I waited on the footpath, arms crossed. Resentful, impatient. Everything she wore blended, a forest of colours drawing your eye into it until it landed on one thing that she had placed just so - the statement piece, she would explain. Which always led the eye to her face, its seamlessness, and you realise you have been staring at her for quite a while. Today, the one thing was a necklace, a luminous half stone hanging on the side rather than the middle – poised, like a question – glistening in the just-past-midday sun. A quarter moon rising.

At last she stood next to me, raising her face to the bolt-blue sky for a moment, eyes closed (settles the face, moistens the make-up she had explained), and then both of us squared our shoulders, eyes straight ahead, walking towards the beautiful sandstone walls which were edged with man-high razor wire, casting jagged shadows that quickly cut over and absorbed our own.

We entered the prison, which seemed innocent enough at first – offices piled in on each other, a line-up of people who never caught your eye, shuffling of papers from somewhere behind the thick glass separating ordinary people from official people.

'Do you think they are treating him well?' Daphne asked – rhetorically, I assumed. 'Do you think he is safe? What about food, is he eating well?'

I shrugged.

'What does he look like? Did he look healthy when you last saw him?' Her statement piece jangled a little as she twiddled it with her fingers, moving in the line, avoiding contact with anyone or anything. 'I'm serious,' she whispered harshly in my ear while smiling at no one in particular.

'You don't care, do you?' She said accusingly.

I shrugged. She let out a breath of exasperation, eyes resting on my skirt, and whispered, 'zip, zip', and I quickly closed the tiny bit left open-mouthed at the side of my waist.

'Have you been nice to him when you see him?' This time it was an accusation. We were suddenly in a small cluster of seating and quickly sat. No one else around.

'No, Daphne, I have been horrible,' I said, inspecting my finger where the zipper had bit into it. 'I rush around the whole state, visiting him in whatever Godforsaken place they have sent him to – this is prison number five, by the way – going through this demeaning process each time, always with the specific aim of being horrid to him, close up.'

Daphne crossed her arms and long legs, the movement revealing a swathe of calf, knee and thigh, as her crossover skirt slit open in a long V shape. I looked around us - we were now in a small waiting room; we had been through a series of them, each time being funnelled deeper into the prison, antechambers so tight only two people at a time could go through. These tiny rooms served as a way of keeping visitors apart from each other, examining them more thoroughly through the cameras perched high above and at the sides of the room, asking questions, name, purpose of visit, blah, blah, at the neck of each portal. A hefty cough, full of phlegm, came over the speaker, followed by an announcement that seemed to be read out, syllable by syllable. 'Silence is to be maintained in the waiting room.' Then a pause. Followed by a 'Please.' Daphne held her slim hand to her throat, recoiling. 'This is horrible,' she whispered under her breath.

'No talking, please,' said a second voice from somewhere indiscernible. We looked around. It seemed to be in the room with us but nobody else was there.

'At least they don't have sniffer dogs,' I muttered.

'What?' she said sharply. 'Dogs?' She does this - starts getting alarmed when she wants to slow things down. It's as if she wants to deliberately not understand what is going on.

'I said, no talking, please,' came the voice again, and another rich, ripe cough, arduously teasing out mucous from the innermost reaches of this man's lungs.

My whispering became more urgent. 'And I send him money every week for food. Every week.' She looked at me sideways, hands raised and mouthed 'what?' Then, 'Why every week?'

'He isn't allowed to have more than sixty dollars at any one time.'

Daphne quickly uncrossed her legs, covering them up again with swift precision, having detected a more than casual interest by a couple of guards looking through the glass panels of an adjoining watch-room.

'Why do you have to send him money for food, don't they feed them here?'

I breathed out harshly in exasperation. 'Most prisoners are malnourished, Daphne. The quality of food is low, it's like eating cafeteria food every day.' I hated it when we got into these roles. Cold-hearted, narrow eyed, bitch sister and the startled, wide-eyed, lovely one.

'Well, is sixty dollars enough?' She pleaded.

'The limit. It's the limit, ' my voice scraped my throat. 'Obviously.' I added while she furrowed her brow, causing a small sparkle of eye shadow to glow in the fluorescent light above.

'Obviously?' she asked breathily.

It used to be that I was the interpreter for everyone in the family. I was even loaned out to family friends. English to Greek, Greek to English. One confused face to another. Doctor to patient. Teacher to parent. Me in the middle, interpreting. I didn't like it then, and I didn't like it now.

I didn't answer straight away but indignation won over, and the desire to block her escape into, what was it, innocence. Yes, innocence. Ha. 'Drugs, bribery, exerting power in prison ...' I spat. 'Shall I go on?' I turned in my seat to face her, half smile, not innocent.

Daphne started to deliberately not listen, turning away, looking in the distance, seeing, it seemed, beyond the finger-grimed gyprock walls. For a moment I wanted to reach out and touch her face, the bit where it curved from her cheekbone down to her chin. I don't like being sad. Angry is better. And anyway she suddenly moved and turned to me.

She took a deep breath, shook her head and started another line of chat. 'You have to provide him with encouragement,' she said, hands now crossed piously in her lap. 'And love.' She added, 'Yes, encouragement and love,' nodding approvingly at her own words. 'He is our father after all, you know.' I started to look around the room, the cameras high up in the corners of the room, eyes on stalks trained on us.

Big Brother's voice had gone silent. Maybe the guards were hoping for another glimpse of Daphne's legs.

'He has been through so much,' she said.

'Sweet Jeeesus,' It came out the side of my mouth and I slid into the black vinyl seat, lowering my head.

'Maybe he is ready to be sorry for what he has done,' she said. 'Maybe after all he has gone through with that other family, maybe he is ready to see how lucky he is. To have us.'

She sat up straight, posing, veering to the side of the chair just a little as if a photographer were somewhere in front.

'Do not argue with him,' she said, raising one hand, palm outwards in front of me. 'Be peaceful,' finger pointed at me, instructing, 'and make this a good visit. Something, you know, to comfort him when he is alone with the other prisoners.' I was losing interest - and started studying the people being channeled into the next chamber through the glass walls. 'Remember, this is the first time I have seen him for years.' Not sure if she was talking to me or herself now. But that last thing caused me to straighten in the sighing thin-foamed seat. This was true. We had spoken about him on our constant phone calls, and I had seen him during the trials, but Daphne had been in the US and had not seen him – well, not since Mama had died, all that time ago. I remember Daphne boarding the plane, and looking over my shoulder even as she was hugging me goodbye, hoping He had turned up.

We waited and on hearing a horn, and another command from the speaker system we moved again.

Now we were in another much larger room, grimy white coffee tables and lightweight plastic chairs. The visiting room. Some of the tables were occupied by small groups huddled together, visitors waiting on an inmate yet to be released into the area. We were one of those. Sometimes when the prisoners were aggressive, the guards delayed the visit. An elderly couple – soft, wearied, respectable – sat quietly with their hands in their laps. A young woman with two young kids, settling them in, giving them a packet of chips ripping the plastic, spilling the yellow crinkles as they wriggled.

I was inspecting my nails and then noticed Daphne's pose falter. Dad came out dressed in the regulation bright orange overalls; the colour made his olive skin look strange, and his green eyes look dull. Daphne stood up, breathing heavily, tense.

Daphne held out her hand in some weird gesture - was it like Yoda in Star Wars - reeling out wisdom? I rolled my eyes but then caught sight of her wrist. One small word tattooed there. 'No', in black edges harsh and bright even after all these years. It had been her favourite word, the one she used most when we fought him. I rubbed my own wrist. 'God'. That was my word. Because it was the only other being who could have authority over Him, Dad. I smiled remembering Daphne's spitting rages. Daphne and I fought back like caged animals; the lion and the tiger he called us. Louise, our youngest sister, didn't. Or couldn't. Louise was so sweet. Louise was so quiet, her neat ways and folding hands. Louise, shy as a flower, one of those flowers that only turn to the sun when it is out and bright and other times just fold up and stay hidden. Like Mama had been.

I cannot remember what was said between Daphne and Dad on that day in Goulburn jail, but it was the same, same as many conversations I had seen way back when we were growing up. I can't remember those, either. I had forgotten even that I had forgotten. I was watching Daphne and remembered the mock Victorian mirror in our 'olde world charme' hotel that morning. How Daphne had straightened my skirt, pushing it down hard over my hips and thighs, like mama used to. It never sat straight, her lips would press together, and 'it must sit straight,' Mama would mutter.

So I did not hear Daphne's words. It looked like a mime. I saw my sister speak quietly at first, reaching towards him, her body forward – reaching, hoping, eyes soft. And then things changed. I saw her neck strain. I saw her raise her hand to make a point, puncturing the air with a finger over and over. I saw her hold her hands to her head, clawing at her temples and hair as if in pain. I saw her close her eyes and hold back a sob, almost a sob, I thought it was going to be a sob. But instead, she gritted her teeth, straightened herself up in her chair, pulling herself away from its back. She balanced there for a moment. She stood up, a hard standing up, and walked away with precision, measuring each footstep, spitting out the words, 'Let's get out of here,' almost under her breath. I looked around, people were starting to notice, and this was a crew that was used to turning away and noticing nothing. What had I missed? Who cares?

We walked out into what was left of the day. The sky was a crisp blue that stung the eyes a little with its sharpness, and Goulburn's sandstone buildings were lit a fiery deep gold by the angle of the sun. Daphne slammed the car door as she sat in the passenger seat, crossing her arms; sharp scissor-like intake, exasperated rush of outbreath, again and again.

We sat in silence for a moment, an early moon had risen, just to the side of that umbrella of a sky arching above us, poised. For a moment I thought I saw shame sheet across her face, or maybe it was me, mine. I don't know.

I waited for a few moments before driving off, the sky darkening fast, and then took us to a pub we had earmarked beforehand. We always planned things, no matter how many times life took over. The planning ... it helped.

We got out in silence. The sun screamed a little as it fell over the horizon, clutching at the sky dragging at it, the sky smudged red.

The moonlight had sliced the sky into layers. A quarter moon, sharp as a knife, impossibly still and silent. We walked into the pub, and the noise and warmth and chatter hit us like a slap. We sat ourselves near a large lit fire, with friendly talk and guffawing all around us. We still hadn't spoken when I said, 'So,' just to crack the block of silence between us. I kept smiling happily, just to annoy her, I think. She was looking away.

'So. I'm glad you gave me such a fine example of how to be kind and loving to Dad. So that I can learn. You know, for next time when you aren't here to show me how.'

I sat back, drinking in the sounds, the fresh air washed by wood-smoke and burning logs. Daphne sat legs crossed, arms crossed, her face turned in profile to the fire, every muscle tuned hard. I, on the other hand, was feeling a bit joyous. Torment over. Time for fun. I had always recovered quickly. Daphne had always held on tight.

'Do you think you can write down some instructions for me? Because, on reflection, I think I lost some of the finer points, dazzled as I was by your warmth and ... wisdom, patience, and ...'

I could have gone on for ages, and would have, but she finally put her hand up and I dramatically ceased as if the gesture had gagged me into silence.

'Look, just get us a drink will you,' she said.

I stood up – looked at her seriously for a moment, hands on the table, and leaned over to her.

'Red or white?' I asked.

She looked up at me, studied me for a second.

'Vodka,' she said. 'Grey Goose, if they have it. But whatever other shit they have if they don't.'

We both smiled. I reached over and mussed her hair, and she batted me away, smoothing her hair back down.

'You are a bitch,' she said.

'Someone has to be,' I said, throwing the words over my shoulder as I headed for the bar.

THE END

Conchita GarSantiago has taken various courses in writing and joined a few writers groups. She has participated in another anthology and published a few short stories in magazines - one was awarded best of the year - and has published in several internet sites. She has also written a historical fiction novel set in the Spanish Civil War titled "A Cry for Home."

Aunty Tessa

Conchita GarSantiago

Queen among the peasants and objectionable among upper-middle class, that was my Aunty Tessa, as I remember her from the early seventies when I was a child. With no children of her own and no responsibilities to burden her.

Whenever she came to our home, I'd run behind mum's skirt and I'd look at her with aversion. I don't think she was even a bit bothered that I, her only niece, the only daughter among five children that my father had, would like her or dislike her. She never asked me for a kiss or for that matter never asked me for anything at all.

When I was seven, at the start of the Spanish summer in mid-June, she fancied having me with her, for the whole long school holidays that lasted until September.

Not having a say in the matter, I looked at my mother as she was packing a few things for me.

'You're going to have a good time,' she reassured me. I didn't answer.

My uncle was the first one to go downstairs, then my aunt. I stood still at the front door of our flat. My mother kissed me on my right temple and lightly pushed me. 'Come on! Don't hold them back.'

Their car was waiting for us, a few meters away from our street's front door. A few of my little neighbours were looking at the shiny car doors. They could see their reflection being short and wide and were making different poses and laughing at it. One of them had the odd idea of blowing her breath into the silver handle of the door, which in turn, made it foggy.

My uncle ran to his vehicle. 'Silly girls! Go away from my car!' Getting his handkerchief out of his pocket, he polished the handle with it until the handle was again bright as a mirror.

I sat in the back of their car mute, while my uncle drove and Aunty sat next to him. I looked through the back window and saw my friends running behind us, waving at me and shouting goodbye.

'This girl doesn't talk much. Does she?' I wondered if my uncle knew what my name was.

'What do you want her to say?' I wasn't quite sure if Aunty Tessa was coming to my rescue or she was implying that whatever I had to say wouldn't be important.

'Are you keen to see my house?' She looked back at me. 'Yes, madam.' Not an honest answer. Probably polite.

After a few long roads, separating the big town and each one of the small towns we crossed, when the light of the day was fading, we entered Medina, where they lived. Just a few streets inside the town, we turned into a straight small road with no street lights. At both sides of the street were huge metal doors all in different pale blue-grey colours against a dirty white wall. With the dusk light, they all looked like giant mouths, ready to eat cars.

My uncle stopped in front of one of these doors. They both got out and after he opened the lock of a small door, my aunt unlocked a big lock inside and the hefty door opened slightly in the middle. They put their hands in the gap and slid the doors apart until it was wide enough for the car to go through. The garage was massive.

There was a big cream and light green coach. On the side of the wheel, it had a half door, just for the driver. Opposite to it was a full size, heavy, metal, manual door, for all the passengers to get in and out of the bus. Standing there, in front of that huge mobile machine I felt little. My mouth dropped.

'Hadn't you seen your uncle's bus before?'

'No. I didn't know he had a bus.'

'Your mother didn't tell you that your uncle has a bus and a taxi?'

"My mother had to tell me my uncle has a bus. Why?" I kept that thought inside my mind.

She carried on talking. 'That's why we bought this big garage.'

I didn't listen to her anymore. I was just looking around. In the middle of the floor was a wooden pit trap. I could see the depth through each one of the pieces of wood.

'Always avoid walking there!' My Uncle spoke to me for the first time. 'It's about a meter and a half deep. You could get hurt if you fell in there.'

'What is it for?'

'To fix things underneath the car or the bus!' Aunty Tessa said quickly. And followed with. 'What do you care about it anyway? Your uncle told you not to get close to it!'

The thought of somebody being there with a huge bus above him gave me an intense feeling of claustrophobia and terror.

At the end of the garage was a very small patio with a few hens. I remember the peculiar smell but couldn't describe it. I can't even say if it was good or bad. It just smelled.

We walked to the end of the street. When we turned the corner, a row of little terrace houses appeared in front of us, looking as if they were holding hands with each other. They were all two stores high, but each one had a different look. Some facades were painted, white, cream or pale yellow, some others were brick. My Aunt's was brick in a pale colour and very small with a big prominent grout between every single brick. Although there were two stories, only the top one belonged to them.

The flat had two bedrooms, a kitchen, toilet and sitting room. The main bedroom and sitting room overlooked a main through road, the way we came. The windows for the second room, bathroom and kitchen overlooked the back, where there was a roof. At the edge of the roof, you could see the end of a patio.

The main through road wasn't only the main road to the little town but it was a main road in Spain. The road that drove you from Madrid to Coruña, in the northwest of Spain. Just over five hundred kilometres long.

The following morning I dared to inspect the cupboard in the room where I was sleeping.

'Oh,' A plastic window in a cardboard box revealed a dreaming doll. Long blond hair, blue eyes and pink cheeks, with arms extended as if she wanted to be picked up. As I was reaching out to the precious box, the bedroom's door opened.

'Ah! You're awake!' Aunty Tessa stepped in. 'It's very late, but I let you sleep in because it's your first day here. From tomorrow you have to get up at eight thirty to have breakfast with me.'

She had a glass of milk in her hand and left it on the tall and dark dressing table. 'Here. Have this milk. Lunch will be soon and if you have a big breakfast you won't eat. It'll be only you and me, today. Your uncle is away with the taxi.'

I didn't say a thing. She looked at me and saw that I was pushing the doll's box inside the cupboard.

'What are you doing?' Silently I looked at her eyes. My hands were touching the doll's box. 'Oh! Well! You can play a little bit with it but be very careful not to break it. It's for Carolina.'

'Carolina?'

'Yes. A neighbour. Her mother is my friend,' said Aunty Tessa as she walked out.

I carefully took the box out of the cupboard and sat it on the tall dressing table that reached to my neck. I stretched myself slightly and rested my elbows on the edge, staring longingly at the beautiful doll until Aunty Tessa called me for lunch. Reluctantly I left the bedroom with the doll still on the dresser.

In the afternoon Aunty Tessa took me to a shop.

'Good afternoon Señora Tessa.'

'Good afternoon Señor Carlos. I've brought my niece. Do you have any proper dress for her, so we can take her outside the house?'

My happiness of having a new dress was quickly clouded by the assumption of me not having anything decent enough to wear.

The man came out from the back a few minutes later with a blue and white dress. My eyes glowed when I saw it. But, my Aunt's didn't.

'Huh. I don't know. Do you have any other?'

'I like this one.' My voice was loud enough to be heard.

'Nobody has asked for your opinion!' She didn't even look at me as she said so.

Nine dresses were lying on the shop counter. I was still looking at the first one and touching it lightly with my fingertips.

'Put your hands up.'

'What?'

'Your hands up, girl!' She lowered her hands to my knees, and as they rose upwards my dress came with them.

'We have fitting rooms there.' The man of the shop said. My aunt ignored the comment and put the pink dress on me.

'I don't like it.'

'Again. Did anybody ask you?'

It wasn't that I didn't really like it, but out of all those, it was the one I liked least.

'Ok. This one and that one.' She pointed to the one I had on and another beige one.

We arrived home and I had not said a word. After putting the two big boxes containing the dresses on top of my bedroom's cupboard, we went to have dinner.

I was slowly filling my spoon with the soup and savouring it with each spoonful.

'Come on! Are you going to finish that soup?' I looked at her and tried to eat faster.

'I'm not going to wait for her. Give me the main course.' My uncle's tone was as unpleasant as his words.

When I finally finished my soup a plate with a steak sat in front of me. I'd have gone to bed very happy with just the soup, but I didn't dare say I didn't want to eat the steak. I cut a very small piece.

'Don't mess with me!' I looked at her with big eyes, a bit scared and a bit shocked.

'Cut those pieces in a normal size!' As she said this she cut a piece I thought was too big. 'Eat it!' The piece of steak was on her fork one centimetre away from my mouth. I found it very chewy and couldn't eat it. But taking it out of my mouth was out of the question. So there I was. Chewing and chewing.

'Oh, God! This is too much for me. I'm out of here!' My uncle threw his serviette on the table and walked away. My aunt didn't say anything but the way she looked at me said it all.

The following morning, I didn't want to leave my room. I just stood again longingly looking at the doll inside the box.

'Aren't you going to come out to have breakfast?'

'I'm fine, in here.'

'What are you talking about? You have to eat.'

To my surprise, breakfast was delicious, although it was just a piece of bread with butter and jam and a hot chocolate.

'A girl will be coming, later on, to take you out to play.'

'Carolina?'

'No. Not Carolina.'

'Why not?'

'Well she's... she is... she is too old for you.'

'How old is she?'
'She's going to be nine.'
'I've got a friend who's nine.'
'Never mind. You'll go with Rosa.'
Rosa was a cheerful outspoken girl.
'This is my niece. I told you she'd be coming.' 'Hello! My name is Rosa.'
'Hi. My name is Aurora.'
'Okay. Off you go to play outside.'

I wanted to show Rosa the doll I found in my room. I hesitated at the door if to tell Rosa to come to my room, but looking at my aunt, I thought she wouldn't allow it.

We ran and we yelled and we laughed and I went back home happy .

Until dinner time when something similar to the previous night happened.

But while I was feeling inconsequential, I was thinking as soon as I finished I'll be back in my room looking at the beautiful doll.

And there she was, standing on the dressing table, waiting for me. In the following days, it became a religious statue, that you were supposed to kneel in front of and start to pray.

It was Saturday afternoon. Despite the calendar telling us it was summer, there were a few great white clouds scudding across the blue sky and the wind was turning cold.

My Aunt entered my room. 'Here! Time for you to wear one of your new dresses.'

'Why?'
'Because you're coming with us.'
'Rosa is coming.'
'You're not going with Rosa today. You're coming with your uncle and me.'

I wanted to go with Rosa but I didn't dare to say anything. After putting my new dress on, I took my light cardigan and walked out of the room.

'What are you doing with that cardigan?'
'It's a bit cold.'
'Take it off! Your dress won't be seen underneath that!'

The three of us went to sit in a cafe.
'We will buy you an ice cream. You'll like that won't you?'
'Yes, madam.'
'Sure you will.'
'Tessa! Nice to see you!' A woman my aunt's age approached our table.
'Sofia! What are you doing here? Do you want to sit with us?'
'No, thank you. I'm just here to look for my friend Raquel.'
'I haven't seen her.'
She swooped into the cafe with her eyes. Then she checked her watch. 'I think I'm a bit early.'
'Well, sit with us for now. You're not going to be on your own.'
'Ok. Thanks.' She looked at me. 'Who's this nice little girl?'
'My niece! My brother's daughter. You remember my brother, don't you?'
'Sebastian! Sure I do! How old is she?'
'She's seven.'
'Seven?'
'Stand up!' Aunty Tessa commanded me.
'Oh! She's very tall for seven! And what a beautiful dress!'
'I bought it! And another beige one!'
'How nice to have such a generous aunt!' She looked at me and I shyly smiled.
Aunty made a gesture with her hand and I sat down. My ice cream arrived on a plate, together with their drinks.
'Do you want to have anything, Sofia?' My uncle spoke for the first time.
'No, thank you Paco. I'll wait for Raquel.'
Just as she finished saying this another lady stood by our table. 'Oh! Raquel. You're here!'
'I'm not late. Am I?' Then she looked at my aunt. 'Tessa. Lovely

to see you, I haven't seen you in ages...' Then she looked at me and again the same conversation about me and my dress. I decided to ignore them and eat my ice cream.

'Excuse me. They're talking to you!' Aunty Tessa yelled at me.

"No, they are not talking to me. They're talking about me, but they're talking to you." I wanted to say. But instead, I put my spoon down and I looked up to the lady. After what seemed an eternity the two ladies left.

My ice cream was melting. I ate with the spoon from the little block that remained there, but the thickness of the spoon couldn't scoop the melted ice cream. I helped it with my finger.

My aunt was shocked. 'Doesn't your mother teach you good manners?'

The following morning I had to go to church with my uncle and aunt. An occasion to wear the other one of the new dresses. In the afternoon I was out with Rosa again. Needless to say, going with Rosa and her friends didn't qualify for me to wear either of my new dresses. Just as well, since I arrived home covered in dirt.

The front door was open. I heard some voices as I walked in. I stepped into the sitting room. I saw a lady slightly shorter than Aunty Tessa and quite overweight. Her dyed blond hair was tied up in the back of her head in a voluminous bun. Her brown eyes were shadowed with intense blue eye colour and her lips covered with bright red. She was wearing a smart green summer dress and white high heel shoes. Her wrist, fingers and ear lobes were busy with thick gold. To her left was a little girl more or less my height. The girl's hair was long and fair. She had it loose down her back and it was glossy and healthy. I thought I recognised her dress from Señor Carlos' shop. She had a tiny gold bracelet on her right wrist. When she spotted me at the door of the room, she looked at me with disgust. So did the mother .

Aunty Tessa, who had her back to me and was blocking part of my view of the girl, turned around.

'Where have you been?' She was embarrassed and furious.

'We went to play in the caves.'

'He he.. Children...' The lady said with a false smile. The girl didn't change her look.

'I'm glad you liked Zaragoza and you enjoyed your holidays and that you're back home, safe and sound.' Aunty Tessa said, probably wanted them to go, so she could tell me off. The lady smiled at Aunty and then she looked at her daughter.

I saw some wrapping paper on the table and aunty had a small silver figurine of the virgin of Pilar, (The matron of Zaragoza), in her hands.

'Alright. Carolina, dear, say thank you to Tessa,' I moved, so my aunt wasn't between me and Carolina. On the other hand, I saw she was holding a big bag.

Panicking, I ran to my room. The top of my dressing table was empty. The whole room felt empty! The precious doll was in that bag.

I didn't care at all when at dinner, aunty was telling her husband how I arrived "bathed in dirt" while Carolina was looking like a shiny coin.

Being a taxi driver with his own taxi, Uncle Paco could come home whenever he wanted. Most days he ate lunch with us. Both of them finished their lunch in a snap. Uncle Paco went back to wait for clients in need of a taxi, Aunty Tessa started to do the washing up while I was eating my last bits on the plate.

'Come on, bring me all the dirty dishes from the table.'

Still munching I obeyed. In a distracted way, I looked out the window and saw the line of the lower roof and the last bit of the patio. Suddenly a snout came into my view. Then, two eyes. It went back and forth again. I stood on a chair holding myself with my hands on the top frame of the window, leaning over.

'What are you doing?' She came to me holding me by my waist. I was still astonished at the sight. 'What creature is that?'

She didn't answer me. Just yelled and told me how I could have gone over the window. At dinner time she told her husband and the two of them were laughing out loud.

'They're not pigs in the city?' Uncle Paco laughed looking at me.

'I thought pigs were pink. That one was grey.'

They carried on laughing and let me with the wonder how those pink beautiful pigs I used to colour in my book could have that ugly colour.

After a few weeks my aunt asked me to sit with her.
'We're going on an excursion tomorrow, Saturday.'
'Oh! Where are we going?'
'Not you. You'll stay here with señora Maria. You know, the neighbour three doors down!'
'Why?'
'Your uncle has to take the local basketball team to Madrid. They're playing a match there and I have to go with him, so while he's driving the coach I'll be selling the tickets for the seats. Señora Maria will come in the morning and take you to her house. I'll make an omelette for you, so she doesn't have to cook anything extra.'

The following morning I was woken up by señora Maria.
'Come on Aurora. Get up. We have to go to my place.'
Still half asleep I walked into the kitchen, rubbing my eyes.
'Your aunt said she cooked an omelette for you, but I can't see it.'
'She put it on a plate outside the window for it to cool down.'
Señora Maria picked up a plate 'This plate? There are only crumbs on it!'
We looked out and we saw a cat on the lower roof, licking its lips.
'How could your aunt be so thoughtless? With all the cats we have around here!' Then, she took me to my room. 'Get dressed. You'll eat with us. I told her she didn't need to cook anything for you!'
Eating with them I felt at home. Four solid, big boys sitting at the table, señora Maria and her husband.

The couple were talking among themselves. 'Old Teodosio was in the bar today.'

'Our bar?'

'Of course, our bar.'

'Oh! It's been a long time since he's come into our bar.'

'He joined in with the other old men to play cards.'

'Well. I'm glad he came.'

'Well, I'm not. The cards weren't the classical ones. They had drawings of animals and suddenly one of the other oldies said, "look, I think this is a wombat. Sounds familiar?"

He went furious! Two chairs were broken.'

Somehow the words came to my mouth. 'What's a wombat?'

'She was listening.' Señor Pío murmured to his wife, but left me thinking why it was so important that a playing card had a drawing that was called "wombat". Why did that drawing provoke an old man to break two chairs?

Then, the second oldest boy slapped his younger brother and after the poor boy cried out, everybody started screaming at each other .

'Enough!' Señora Maria's husband's voice was loud and authoritarian. Silence was restored. I looked up and the same boy winked at me, with a witty smile.

The weeks that followed up until the end of summer, when I had to return home, weren't very different. Outside games with Rosa and her friends, suffering dinners with my aunt and uncle, ice cream with them on Saturday afternoon and mass on Sunday morning.

I was packing to go home. Aunty Tessa came into the room, just at the moment, I was putting my new dresses into my suitcase.

'What are you doing?'

'Packing.'

'Not these!' She said as she took the new dresses and hung them back in the cupboard.

∼

Next June arrived, Aunty Tessa was again at our home, to take me with her. Mum thought I was having some kind of summer holiday that she herself and my father couldn't give me.

She was ignorant about the precious doll, the "majestic" Carolina, who was too elegant to be my friend and my misery at mealtimes. Not about the new dresses. She knew about that as soon as Aunty Tessa put her first foot in my home, the previous year when she came to bring me back.

'I had to buy her two dresses. Two! She didn't have anything decent to wear.'

Mum kept silent. I felt very sorry for her, but I didn't know what to say either.

The prospect of spending another summer with my uncle and aunt didn't give me any pleasure, but in the past summer, Rosa had become my best friend. I was eager to see Rosa again and the price for seeing her was to spend the summer with uncle and aunt and go along with the "show" to friends and neighbours about how much aunty Tessa cared for me.

The first Saturday I was there, I already knew the routine, I went to put one of the "new" dresses on and they were extremely tight.

'You'll have to wear it.'

'I can't breathe.'

'Don't exaggerate!'

When I was sitting at the cafe with them, having my ice cream, I made a movement with my arms and shoulders and the bottoms at the back jumped out. I thought Aunty Tessa would be mad but to my surprise, she laughed out loud.

For the following Saturday afternoons and Sunday mornings. I used the same dresses... just open at the back. I had to put a cardigan on top. Either it was slightly cold, which hardly was, or hot, which was most of the days.

As always, at every meal, they finished eating before me.

'I'm full and done. I'll be gone.' Uncle Paco was leaving the table.

'Just rest for a few minutes.'

'I can't. I have a trip just now.'

'You mean with the taxi!'

'Of course, with the taxi. We haven't organised any excursions.'

'Where are you going?'

'I have to take Señor Montijo to Avila, to see his brother.'

'Why doesn't he take the train?'

'He's rich enough to go by taxi and that's good for us.'

'Can the girl and I come with you?'

'Yes, but you'll have to sit in the front seat. He's paying for the trip so you can't bother him.'

I was sitting on my aunt's lap while the car was waiting at the door for Señor Montijo. When uncle Paco saw him come out of the door, he went out to help with the luggage. Very clumsily, the old man sat in the back.

'Oh! We have company!'

'This is my wife, Tessa and this is my niece.'

We both said hello.

'The little girl can sit in the back with me!'

'She's fine here!' The two of them said in unison.

'Honestly. It's not a problem. She can sit here.'

'Don't bother yourself, please,' Aunty Tessa said.

The man was talking incessantly, about his brother, him being single... and every now and then as if it were the chorus of a song he'd say, 'Honestly, the girl could sit in the back with me.' And carrying on with the "chorus" the answer would always be. 'Please don't bother yourself.'

About one hour later and a full narrative of his simple life, we arrived at the town of Avila, where we left Señor Montijo.

'Shall we have a walk or a drink, here in Avila?' Uncle asked. 'Nah! We'll only spend money.'

I was about to ask why we came when Aunty Tessa looked back at me. 'You may look at the famous wall of Avila.'

I have to confess that it did impress me. A medieval wall surrounding the whole town stood there, longer than my eyes could see.

As we were arriving at Medina. I saw a sign saying "Tordesillas 10 km."

'Oh! That's Tordesillas! My brother Antonio is staying in a camp there. Maybe we could visit him!'

Aunty Tessa turned back to me. 'Will you pay for the petrol to take the detour?' I was simply muted.

The weeks up to September didn't bring any new activities or ventures and after spending the whole school year at home, I was anxious to resume my summers with Rosa and her friends.

I heard Rosa's cheerful voice from my room and ran to the door. Her sparkling eyes, open smile and red cheeks made me feel good.

'We're going to go dancing in the community hall. They put up some coloured lights and have music. It's going to be such a blast!'

'You're too young to go to the dance!' My aunt was shocked. 'Everybody's going. All ages.' Rosa was assertive.

'In the community hall?' I asked. For me the community hall was a place for talks and for groups of young people to show their abilities as singers, instrument players and actors. But I never saw one made into a discotheque. 'How odd!'

'Well, here we use the hall for everything.' Rosa was quite proud about her local arrangements. 'It costs two pesetas. (Two cents)'

'I have to give you two pesetas?' Aunty Tessa didn't like that part.

'Well, that's... just the entry fee. But we'll have a drink as well' Rosa was braver than me.

'You'll have a drink when you come back.' Aunty Tessa said, looking at me. Rosa could be very brave, but my aunt wasn't going to be defeated. Even if it was for a few pesetas.

'Here' She put two pesetas in my hand. 'But don't you think I'm going to give you money every day!'

'Come on. Let's run.' Rosa was probably scared that she'd take the coins back.

We met with Rosa's friends, Maria, Pilar and Angeles.

'Come on. Let's go buy some chewing gum before the dance starts.' We all went to the kiosk and I stayed a couple of steps behind.

'Here! I bought two!'

'Thank you, Rosa.' I was very grateful to her, but I felt quite ashamed because she was more generous with me than my aunt was.

As we walked down the street, we were happily chewing and making bubbles.

'Let's see who makes the biggest bubble!'

Between laughs and silly jokes, we arrived at the hall. A long line of young and not so young people were excitedly waiting to enter. Many children our age were trying to cut into the line. The happy music coming from inside made everybody bop before entering.

As we came inside, a lady said hello to Rosa.

'I thought I'd see you here...'

'Hello, Aunt Alicia.' (Not her real Aunty, as she'd tell me later).'I said to my husband you'd be here. And with your three friends. Oh! today you have four friends.'

'Yes. This is Aurora. Aurora is from Valladolid.'

'Ah! A city girl, eh?' She looked at me with a sweet face. I smiled.

'She's Paco and Tessa's niece.' Rosa clarified.

'Is that so?'

'Yes, Madam.' Not that I felt proud about it.

'The ones with the coach... My husband and I went with them to Segovia last year, just before summer.'

She opened a bag and got a big packet of crisps out. 'Here enjoy them!'

'Thank you, Aunty Alicia.' Rosa kissed her and we all said thank you and goodbye.

'Off you go! Have fun!' She walked away.

'What are we going to do with the chewing gum? Mine still has flavour.' I asked.

'Mine too. Don't worry. Come here.' They all ran to the entrance. Next to the front door, there was a long piece of timber, nailed to the greyish, filthy wall and from it a few hooks stuck out. Many people had hung their jackets there. The four girls slipped underneath the jackets and stuck their chewing gum on the wall. 'There will be safe,' Rosa said.

'Mine is the one under the pink jacket.' Angeles made sure nobody would take her gum. I was hesitant.

'Come on!' Pilar yelled at me as she gave me a pat on my back. Reluctantly, I stuck my gum on the plastered filthy wall.

'Ok. Aurora's gum is under the dark green jacket.' To be honest, I wasn't thinking about putting it inside my mouth again.

Everybody was dancing together regardless of their age. A young man around twenty singled me out and was dancing with me. Everybody circled us and my face was red as a tomato.

Just before the dance finished, the organisers had a ruffle. The first prize was a ham, the second prize a salami bar and finally the third prize, they got us in suspense reading the number of our entrance tickets. I had number 158. I couldn't believe my ears when the man finally said, 158. All the girls around me patted me and cheered. The price was one kilo bag of sweets.

I walked back where my friends were with it in my hands, holding it up. I opened it and I gave sweeties to my friends and some other kids around. I was left with half of the bag.

With laughs and full of frenzy, we left the hall.

They all walked with me to my aunt's. Still, with the euphoria of the good time, we couldn't keep down our giggles. Aunty Tessa stepped outside the front door in the street. I knew somehow she'd do or say something nasty about my prize, so as soon as I saw her, I put the bag of sweeties, under my cardigan.

'What do you think you're doing? Coming so late and making such a roar!'

I stepped in and she shut the door without letting me say goodbye.

That summer my aunt and uncle organised a few excursions with people from the town to go to different places.

The tickets were sold in advance and until all the seats were filled, there wasn't any confirmation of the excursion taking place.

Sometimes they even sold four extra places and four travellers had to sit in a folding chair attached to the fixed chairs in the corridor of the bus.

If paying customers could sit in a folding chair, I could sit on the engine. The engine for the bus was next to the driver. A big dark red, paddy leather cap looking like a casket, covered the whole engine and was the special seat for me. To be honest, I didn't mind.

I found it quite diverting. Although now, thinking back, I realise I was lucky that uncle Paco drove slowly, or a brusque brake would have launched me out of the huge window.

The first excursion was to Madrid.

That was the first time I saw the capital of Spain. Its big avenues and busy traffic called my attention. We were walking along "Paseo del Prado". Then, we stopped at the corner with "Plaza de la Cibeles." Plaza de la Cibeles is a big roundabout with the statue of Cibeles in the middle. It has lived there since the eighteenth century surrounded by water. An icon of Madrid, before they built tall, modern and exotic buildings.

Madrid was interesting but would have been better if Rosa had been invited.

She invited me the following day to her house.

Every time I went out with Rosa, I took a few sweets to have during the day. I was happy to have something that was mine, to share with Rosa, even if it was just a bunch of lollies. And happier that my aunt hadn't discovered my little treasure.

Rosa lived in a long quiet street. The feeling of being in the countryside was more palpable than where aunty Tessa lived. All the houses were only one storey, all painted in different colours. At the front door, there was a curtain made of colourful plastic tubes attached to each other top to bottom with a sort of spring. As soon as you touched it all the little tubes that made the curtain danced making a giggling sound. Behind this curtain, there was a thick timber door cut horizontally in the middle. The top door was ajar and the bottom one had a big iron lock. Rosa pushed the top half and leaning over the bottom door, she undid the lock on the bottom one. All the neighbours had the same style of door and whenever anybody was coming in, no matter who they were, they'd open the door in the same way as Rosa did and once in the kitchen. - which was normally the room the front door led to - they'd yell the name of the owner.

'Nobody ever comes to our house, but I told Mum you're a good friend.'

I followed her to the living room. It was a smallish room of about 3.5 square meters.

Rosa's four-year old brother was kneeling on the floor playing with two little cars on the tea table. Rosa's father was sitting at the edge of one of the sofas and there was an old man pacing the room. Hands held together at the back, head down, beret on his head and a cigarette stuck in his dried mouth. Suddenly he stopped and with his big hands, long fingers and yellow nails he took the cigarette out of his mouth at the same time as he stopped, lifted his head: 'Is there anybody with big enough "cojones" who would kill this bastard?'

I was shocked. Everybody ignored me. Only Rosa was aware of my big eyes and the scared look on my face.

'Don't worry. It's just grandpa. He's harmless. Sit over there.'

She left the room and I sat on the sofa where Rosa's father was, as far as I could from Rosa's grandpa and father.

The father was tapping the sofa's arm with his right hand and covering his face with his left one.

The old man started to pace the room again. Another stop. 'Who would kill him?' Just one more step. 'It cannot carry on like this!'

His son was gesturing with his hand and head in a sign of resignation.

'We have to kill him!' Suddenly grandpa's voice was higher. Rosa's father stood up and as he was walking out of the room he said. 'You go and you kill him!'

Despite Rosa's previous reassurance, I was still shocked and scared. I could hear Rosa's mother. 'You know you shouldn't bring people home!'

Rosa came in. 'Is he your gran-pa on your mum's side?'

'No. He's dad's dad. Grandpa Teodosio. Mum's dad is dead.'

'He's not dead, he's downstairs!' The young boy spoke without taking his sight off his toy cars.

'Shut up! He's dead!' Rosa moved her hand as if threatening him.

'No, he's not! I took him breakfast this morning,' he yelled looking at her.

'Shut up! Let's go Aurora.'

I didn't need to be told twice. Once in the street, I could see

Rosa was very upset. I knew I shouldn't speak, even less ask questions but I felt I was going to explode if I didn't. Only one question I thought. 'Who does your grandfather want to kill?'

'Who else? Franco, of course.'

I had many more questions but I thought I would leave them for another time.

That night I couldn't sleep. Suddenly a name came to mind. "Teodosio!" That was the name Señor Pio said that day in their house, two summers earlier. The old man who didn't like wombats and broke two chairs on Señor Pio's bar.

Something fishy was cooking in my best friend's house and I didn't dare to tell anyone. I didn't want to betray her. I thought if I just avoided going to her house I'd be safe.

Uncle had a few more excursions with the big coach. They took me with them. Always sitting on the engine and not allowed to bring Rosa with me.

We went to Segovia, where I discovered the aqueduct that the Romans had left there for us, Salamanca, where there was an atmosphere created by the many students who lived there. We also went to Toledo where we saw the two "different Toledos", the new, which was like any other town, and the old, with its streets so narrow that, not even the sun came in. Walking through those streets, I thought it was dark already, but when we came out of all of them, the Sun was really strong and the streets were bright.

After leaving all the passengers in the main square, we drove to the huge garage. Aunt and I would get out of the coach and after she opened the little door with the key, I used all my strength to push the big doors all the way out so the coach could go in, to sleep.

It was two weeks until the end of summer.

'You finished tidying up your room?'

'Yes.'

'Ok. Let's go. We have to buy groceries.' That was one more burden that Aunt imposed on me.

I suppose it was a relief in a way that the burden was shared with the owner of the little shop where we were buying.

'Tessa, your turn!' I could see the uneasiness on the lady behind the counter.

'Can I have some steaks?'

The lady took a piece of meat.

'Not. I don't want any steak from that one. That other one.' Aunty commanded.

When the lady took the other one, aunty Tessa frowned. The butcher took another piece.

'Oh no! What are you giving me there?'

After the lady showed aunt Tessa a few pieces, she chose from the first one.

The tomatoes, oranges, peaches... weren't saved from my aunt's scrutiny in the fruit shop, either. Nor were the baguettes at the baker's.

As aunty Tessa was opening the lock of the front door, in the street, she looked back 'Oh. Look who's here.'

I was more than ready to go home, so as soon as the door was opened I walked in without looking at that person.

'Hello, Tessa.' I thought I recognised the voice, but I didn't care to think who it could be.

'Hello. How are you?' Aunty Tessa's voice was soft.

'How's your niece?'

'Fine.'

'Does she still have teeth?'

That called my attention.

'What do you mean?' Aunt was intrigued.

'With all those lollies, anybody would lose all their denture!.' The ball dropped. It was Rosa's aunt Alicia. The one I met at the dance.

'What lollies?' Aunt asked.

I ran upstairs and I don't know how, but Aunty Tessa was just behind me.

'Show me those lollies!'

'I...'

'Come on!'

'I...' I have to confess I have never been good at lying. 'I only have a few.'

'You've eaten a kilo of lollies?'

'No. I gave lollies to other kids.'

'Give me the bag!'

That was the last time I saw the lollies. But that wasn't enough. She punished me without seeing Rosa until the last day. Aunty Tessa showed mercy on me and let me go to say goodbye.

This time when she "delivered" me home, the summary of my holidays to Mum was,

'She got one kilo of sweets in a dance she went to. A country dance. Can you believe it? One kilo of sweeties and she didn't have the decency to tell me anything! She just hid them!'

In the fourth year, nobody came to pick me up. I don't know the reason, but I was told that I was to take the train. My father took me to the station in Valladolid.

'You know where you have to get off, don't you?'

'Yes. As soon as I see the castle from the train, I'll stand by the door. - Medina has a medieval castle on top of a little hill. In the sixteen century Juana la loca, (Joan the mad) daughter of Ferdinand and Isabella and sister of Catherine of Aragon, lived and died there. (We studied that at school and made us proud that it was in our province).

You can see the castle from far away.

'Your uncle will be at the station waiting for you with the taxi.' Dad said as I was getting on the train.

How naive of me to think that I was going to be treated like a "lady" (a taxi waiting for me at the station!) When the train arrived at Medina, a lot of passengers got out. There were all the taxi drivers, a total of six, I believe, catching passengers as if they were butterflies.

We were nine people all scrambled inside my uncle's car. Most of them were going to small villages nearby where the train didn't arrive.

∽

The routine of the three previous years didn't change. I was still very happy with my friend Rosa and we played every day that Aunty Tessa allowed it.

The temperatures were shooting up. Adults were constantly complaining, but we children loved every minute of it. Uncaring about sun protection or trying to be in the shade, we'd arrived home with bright red faces.

I was waiting for Rosa when Señora María came in.

'So, Tessa, you have everything ready for tomorrow?'

'I just finished the first omelette. I'm going to make three more.'

'Isn't that too much?'

'I don't think so, we're... two... four... six... twelve people.'
'Aurora, are you coming?' Señora Maria looked at me.

Aunty Tessa beat me to my answer. 'Of course, she is.'

'Coming where?' I was totally unaware of anything that was happening.

'We're all going to a picnic.' Señora María showed me the best of smiles. Then looking at my aunt, 'I'll fry a few chorizos and I'll make a pie with them.'

'Señora Rosario's taking a few salads, Señora Alicia is bringing a meat pie and Señora Paula said she's bringing some baguettes.'

'That's easy...'

'What about drinks?'

'Everybody takes their own.'

Unfortunately for me, Carolina and I were the only girls. Her way of looking at me was exactly the one she had the first time we saw each other when she took "my doll". So, we both ignored each other .

The two youngest boys of señora Maria, were also there. I enjoyed playing with them and I had some fun.

After I played soccer with them, we sat to eat.

'Couldn't you have sat with us, ladies, like Carolina did, instead of playing with the boys?' Aunty Tessa whispered in my ear.

I looked at her but said nothing. After a moment, grabbing the bottle of water, I said, 'I'm thirsty!.'

'Silly me, I forgot to bring glasses.' Aunty Tessa spoke loudly.

'I can lend you one.' One of the ladies offered.

'Don't worry. We'll drink from the bottle.' I was about to do so when Aunty Tessa grabbed the bottle from me.

'Your uncle will drink first. Then, me and then you.'

'I'm going to fish.' One of the men stood up with a fishing pole and started to walk towards the river.

'Those fish are dead! Señor Pio yelled.

'As dead as "el pajero". The man with the fishing pole said.

Everyone laughed.

'Who is el pajero?' I asked softly to the youngest boy.

'Your friend's grandpa.'

A few days later, as we were having dinner I asked what had been going around in my head.

'What does pajero mean?'

Aunty Tessa went red, 'where did you hear that?'

'Somebody said it at the picnic.'

'Oh!' Uncle Paco laughed. 'You mean your friend's grandpa?'

'He was working with "paja" (hey) when he was young.' Aunty explained, then in a serious voice she added, 'Don't you repeat that word to anyone.'

I was puzzled, but the silence at the table told me they wouldn't talk about that anymore.

It was many years later that I learned "pajero" also means wanker. There was something else that had had me wondering many things, for over two years now.

'Is Rosa's grandpa dead?'

'Don't you know?' I suppose aunty wanted to know what I knew. 'Well, I saw an old man once when I went to her house. I never went back. I think his name was Teodosio. But she has another grandpa. Doesn't she?'

'Well, I think you know enough.'

It was in that fourth year that uncle Paco warmed up to me. He taught me the names of the car's models.

We were on the balcony. In front of us was the stretch of the big road that passed by Medina, going from Coruña to Madrid and vice versa, and was always very busy with cars.

'If you tell me all the car's models with no mistake, I'll give you a peseta (one cent)' He said.

'Right, the white one is a Fiat 600.'

'The one behind is a Simca 1500.'

I mentioned at least fifteen without making a mistake.

'Alright. You win. Here's your peseta.'

Right at that moment, aunty Tessa came in. 'What's going on here?'

'Nothing.' We said in unison.

'What do you have in your hand?'

'Nothing.'

'Show me your hand, girl!'

I didn't want to, but she wouldn't give it up.

As I opened my hand, the peseta was in the middle of it. Aunty Tessa took it. 'I'll keep it safe for you.'

The following year, they moved just a few meters along the same road. It was a brand new block of flats opposite a new swimming pool.

The owner of the pool was an acquaintance of aunty Tessa and in a conversation, he said in a polite way, 'you're very welcome to come.' She took it literally. Every single morning she was there without paying a cent for the entrance.

When I was in Medina, she'd take me with her, for the same price. Unfortunately Rosa wasn't invited, but lucky for me there were other kids I could play with. So we jumped into the water, we swam, we played and after a while we came out of the water wet and cold. The other Mums, wrapped their kids in their towel as soon as they came out, so they wouldn't be too cold. Aunty Tessa didn't want me to make the towel damp and asked me to run around until I was dry.

Then, the ladies would give their children a few coins so they could go to buy a packet of chips. So did my aunt. When we returned, all the kids sat on the towels munching their precious chips and I had to give my packet to her. After she had what she wanted, she gave me what was left.

In the new block of flats they had made a park with swings in the centre. We went to the park every afternoon and practiced our acrobatics skills on the swings and we fell onto the ground that was covered with stones. Our tomboy games didn't give us any distress even if we were hurt, we'd go home happy.

It was at that time, that the 83 years old generalissimo, Franco, was very sick, and things started to change. Some of them were very visible. Among others, Medina saw for the first time my friend's "other" grandpa.

He walked along the streets of Medina, squinting a lot and with a big smile on his face

People gathered around him and applauded as if he was on his own poor parade. No balloons, no music, no other people joining him, but I bet he felt like a hero as he waved his hands happily to the multitude.

I saw Rosa among the crowd and went to her. 'What's happening?'

'Grandpa is out.' She looked proud and clapped her hands with enthusiasm. I didn't say a thing. Rosa carried on explaining. 'He's been in the basement for almost forty years.'

Later on, somebody explained to me that some people who had fought during the Spanish Civil War on the side of the Republicans, against Franco, hid after the war finished and their families declared them dead. They were scared to come out and be persecuted. Many of them dug a tunnel under their property or had just a basement and they stayed there for many years. That was the reason they were called wombats.

∼

Once in our teens, we started to see boys in a different way; They weren't there just to pull our hair or try to lift our skirt, any more.

We made an agreeable group of girls and boys.

We learnt to converse, we learnt to flirt, we had our first cigarette and we felt important.

Luckily for me, I was excused from going every afternoon to have my ice cream with my dear aunt and uncle. However, I wasn't excused from fulfilling my obligations with the holy church and had to go to the boring mass every Sunday morning. Uncle and aunty came with me. I could see Aunty Tessa praying with lots of sentiment. It reminded me of something Mum used to say: "I don't say that everybody who goes to church is a bad person, but, that, all bad people do go to church, I have no doubt about it."

The year I was fifteen, I made my way from my parent's flat to my aunt's flat.

When I arrived, she was waiting for me, but she didn't say hello.

'Your mother told me over the phone that you failed two subjects.'

I looked at her without answering.

'Well? Did you bring your books?'

'No...'

'What do you mean no? You failed and you left your books behind?

'There are only two subjects! I have nine all together! I'll leave a few days earlier and I'll study then. I'm sure I'll pass.'

'Carolina already passed all of them with top marks.'

'Sure.' I murmured.

I did go out almost every day and had fun with my lovely group of friends, but aunty didn't let me forget about my exams, any single evening at dinner.

'Why can't you be more like Carolina?' 'I don't want to be like her.'

'Well, she's doing very well at school.'

'Good for her.'

'She'll have a prosperous future, while you... you'll be cleaning people's houses!'

I didn't answer and that infuriated her. She went on praising Carolina and humiliating me more.

Eventually uncle Paco came to my rescue. More or less. 'Let her be! She knows what she's doing.'

'I don't think she does!'

When I finally mastered how to chew all those steaks she cooked, they had to mortify me in a different way!

The year I was sixteen, Rosa gave me big news. 'My family and I are moving to Valladolid?'

'Really?' I hugged her 'That's great news!' We can be together for the whole year!'

'We are moving after Christmas.'

That year, I saw seventeen-year-old Jose Manuel, with different eyes. Truth to be told, everybody did. He had grown at least ten centimetres in the past year. Where there were skinny limbs before, muscles had developed. His blue eyes that were cold and empty, were now profound and intense.

I fell head over heels in love with him. I confessed to Rosa and she was my ally.

We met every afternoon at the benches in the main Plaza of Medina. Rosa always managed to keep a spot for me to sit next to Jose Manuel. We all talked, laughed and had a good time.

One of the eighteen-year-old boys would go to the nearest bar to buy a "porrón" a container for liquid in the form of a "V" with a round base. One of the "v" sides was wide enough to pour the liquid inside, the other one was a sort of cone wide at the bottom and ending in a tiny hole. Through that hole, the liquid came out in a long thread. The liquid was beer and lemonade. We passed it along as we gave a performance of our ability to drink making as long a stream as possible, ending in our mouth.

I did enjoy those afternoons until one fatal day a short girl slightly overweight, stopped by our benches. We all looked at her as if asking "what are you doing here?"

Then, I realised.'That's Carolina!' I whisper to Rosa. Carolina spoke loud and clear, 'Jose Manuel invited me.' With that, she pushed her bum between him and me and happily sat there for the whole afternoon. And... the following afternoons.

I felt like my body was growing spikes. I was so angry!

Her happiness of being next to Jose Manuel didn't bring misery only to me. More people were annoyed at her sitting there, with her silly laugh, posing, flirting and ignoring the rest of us.

Luckily for us, her family had enough money to go every summer to the seaside on holidays for three weeks and when the day of her family's holiday arrived, we recovered Jose Manuel.

I started to speak to him. My flirting was flat. I couldn't flirt like Carolina, but I had the feeling that he appreciated that.

One evening, it was after midnight, which is a normal hour for young people to arrive home- and he said he'd walk with me. My body was alight with glee. We walked along the road where my uncle and aunt lived, but on the opposite footpath. On that way, we had a full view of the balcony. And vice versa!

When we reached the front door and we were saying that timid goodbye, that the two of us knew there was something else to do after the good night words, the door flew open and cursed words were coming out of my aunt's mouth as if they were snakes.

'...Standing here like a little tart with a man at this time of the night! Only whores behave like that. What do you think people are going to think of you?...'

My mouth couldn't articulate any words, my feet couldn't move and my face was red as a tomato. Jose Manuel was in a similar state. Aunt took my arm and dragged me inside, slamming the door at him.

The following morning, I had breakfast in silence. With the same silence I went to my room and packed my things.

'Where are you going?' Aunty was surprised.

'Home.'

'Why? Still a few more weeks for the summer to be over.'

'It is over for me!'

'What are you talking about?'

'I don't want to be here! I have no freedom...'

'No freedom?' She cut me off. 'You do whatever you want!'

'As long as you don't disagree. Like last night!'

'Do you think a well mannered young lady comes home with a man after midnight?'

'We are already in the eighties! Not the forties!' It was at that moment I realised that that was where aunty Tessa had been living. 'I liked that young man!' I said more calmly.

'He is the one who has to go after you! Not you after him!'

'Do you think he's going to come back with me after what you said and how you said it last night?'

'I did that because I love you and I don't want people talking about you!'

'You did that because you love yourself and don't want people talking about your niece in the way you think they'll talk.'

'What are you saying?' 'Goodbye, aunty.'

COMING BACK

The taxi stopped at the front door. I carefully stepped out and tried not to sink my heels inside the cracks of the footpath.

I took a moment to look around. Medina hadn't changed much in the last thirty five years. A cold wind whipped up suddenly and I wrapped myself with my Balenciaga long coat.

I buzzed the bell at the front door, and while I waited for an answer, an excessively fat and short lady passed by.

The door made a noise and as I pushed it opened. Aunty Tessa was at her flat's door waiting for me. 'Well, well, well. About time you came to visit.' 'You know I've been living in Germany.'

'I do. But, you never had time to come to visit?'

'Well, I've been working hard. I had to go to different places, symposiums, talks, seminars.. wherever people needed a language interpretation and translation in Spanish, English or German. I couldn't come to Spain often and when I did, I spent my time in Valladolid, with my family and friends.'

'And I'm not family?' She got angry.

I was about to say, yes you're the nasty member of the family, but who wanted to bring unpleasant things back? Besides, I knew that what she did wasn't out of wanting to be cruel. It was simply the mentality she had. Quite 'in line' with children have to be seen, not heard and children are too young to understand anything or even have feelings. A woman stuck in an era far gone with no children of her own to bring her back to the present day.

She walked to her little sitting room and I followed. She sat at the round table with a long table skirt and I did the same. 'Oh there's a brazier here!' I lifted the table skirt to see it. 'I thought there weren't any more of these things.'

'Plenty of them in Medina. They're very good to warm you up.' We looked at each other in silence for a moment.

'When did you arrive in Valladolid?'

'A few days ago.'

'Where are you staying? When your parents died, your brothers sold their flat.'

'I know. I came for my parents' funeral and for all the papers we had to do later on.'

'You didn't come for your uncle's funeral.'

'It was at the moment my husband was sick. In fact, he died soon after uncle passed away.'

'So, where are you staying?' She repeated. 'In a small hotel.'

'A hotel? Not one of your brothers could put you up?'

'Well, better that way. My sisters-in-law are all very bossy and they'd boss me around.'

'You want me to speak to them? I'll tell them!'

'No. Don't worry. I don't want to make trouble.'

'When are you going back to Germany?'

'I'm not.' She looked at me as if asking why not?

'Well, now that my husband is dead, there's no reason for me to be there.'

'And you didn't have children...'

'I couldn't.' For some reason, I felt angry. 'But I spoiled my nephews and nieces every time they came home.'

'Well, that's what aunts are there for. I treated you like a princess, every time you came.'

'Excuse me?'

'I took you to the swimming pool every day, I bought dresses for you...'

'The first year, later on, you didn't seem to mind what I had in my suitcase.'

She ignored what I said, 'I brought you ice cream every Saturday...'

'When Susana, Antonio's daughter, went near Leeds in England to take a course in English, I was in London with my husband. I took the train to go see her. It took me more than six hours and the ticket was very expensive. I arrived there and I invited her and her friends for lunch. Then we went to a fashion shop and I bought her a top she liked.' I paused. 'Remember when my brother Antonio was in a camp in Tordesillas? Just ten kilometres away from here?'

Once more she ignored me. 'Well, your sister in law must be very happy with you.'

'Actually, she wrote me an angry letter because the top her daughter chose, ran its colours in the washing machine.'

'How does she dare? After all you did for her? I hope you answered her in the way she deserved.'

'I just threw the letter away.'

'Well, I will answer her for you!'

'It was years ago. Let it be!'

In an attempt to change the subject I said. 'When I was downstairs waiting for you to open the door, a woman passed by and I think it was Carolina.'

'It could be. She has never left Medina.'

'She was extremely fat! She wasn't that fat before.'

'She is fat now. She looks like a big ball. And have you seen her husband?'

'I don't know who her husband is.'

'She married a man who had a mechanic's garage.'

'A mechanic?.' I imagined "Majestic Carolina" kissing a man when he's at work full of stains of oil. Then, I felt ashamed of my thoughts. 'Is he the owner of the garage?'

'No. His uncle is. It'll be his when his uncle dies.'

'What does he look like?'

'He's much taller than her and extremely thin. They look like the "l" and the "o" when they go together!' She looked at me. 'She'd be happy if she had half the nice figure and the elegance you have!' She smiled at me for the first time. 'I showed her mother the picture you sent me with your husband. She looked at it but said nothing. She was green with envy.'

"Majestic Carolina," I thought again.

'Well, if you're going to move to Spain, why don't you live here until you find a place of your own? I have plenty of space.'

'Why not?'

THE END

Maree Walk is a Sydney writer who has recently 'come back' to writing. Previously a playwright, Maree is preparing her novel, Modern History, for publication and has authored a few short stories. Maree lives in Sydney

The Brothers Karamazov

Maree Walk

I was in a toilet in a restaurant in Den Haag, Belgium in 1978. I turned to the door and found the lock stubbornly refusing to slip back. The jazz music was loud, plates clattered, and diners talked and laughed so no-one could hear me as I banged on the door. No-one entered the women's toilets either. It was the third time I was locked in a toilet in Europe. At Frankfurt Hauptbahnoff an official looking woman took me seriously and removed the toilet door by methodically unscrewing the hinges and lifting it off. I nodded, *danke, bitte* as I stepped out onto the tiled floor worried it was an overreaction at my behest. I did nearly miss our train down to Florence. I was 19 and travelling with my boyfriend, Stewart.

While I am trying to loosen the lock, I imagine that Stewart's sister, Diana is taking advantage of me in this bloody toilet and, hunching over her wine glass will ask,

"So, how are you two going?" and then she'll put her head on the side, nodding, and add, "You don't seem to be travelling that well."

And I can see Stew leaning back on the chair, stealing a look around, gulping his Heineken, and then whilst Diana, impatiently nods *get on with it*, leans forward, replying,

"No. Not that well."

Diana would be impatient. 'Not that well' is obvious from the stand-off in her lounge room in Cologne, with our packs now at opposite ends of the sofa. When we arrived, at the beginning of our travels, our packs stood together as indeed Stewart and I had.

I took a deep breath and tried again on the door. Stuck. I tried pushing the door and sliding the lock at the same time, and then pulling the door, simultaneously jiggling the lock.

I sat on the toilet lid and began to cry. Not just a few tears, but deep sobs. I tried to stop the noise of my heaving chest, to sob soundlessly, but I couldn't. The barking sobs – like the sound of coughing, but unmistakably crying – echo in the tiny toilet's acoustics. Perhaps it only lasted two minutes, or maybe five. The sobbing released a valve in my chest, but in my stomach, in my gut, there was a stone.

I was feeling stupid a lot of the time, and it didn't agree with me. He's gone cold on me. I can feel him moving away, inching away and the more he does it the more I do that nervous pushing in, crowding him. I am like an Aussies Rules player, *holding the man*.

On the Ponte Vecchio I said, "do you even love me?" It felt the worst of the worse to have to ask. Walking off, embarrassed I even said it, like I'd lost the last of the young woman who boarded the plane in Brisbane with Stew. Gone. A witty feminist he once loved, and now a clingy, whiny adolescent. I blamed him for turning me into that person, but I couldn't see how it actually happened. I hated who I was. I was looking for me.

We are catching trains everywhere zigzagging Europe - the days of the Eurail pass. We board, find a compartment, take our books out of our packs, and put the packs up on the rack above. We're sitting facing each other, and I have my book, The Brothers Karamazov, and start to read. I'm half-way through the second volume in this one thick book weighing down my pack. I have disliked the book ever since the first chapter. I can't work out who is who, the endless names for the characters has me drowning, staring at the page, just seeing letters and words and long sentences. The Brothers

Karamazov is making me feel stupid. I stare at the words thinking *what is wrong with me?* I look over the top of the book and see Stew looking out the window. Sometimes he reads, but often he is sitting, content it seems.

∼

I banged on the door when I heard someone come in. *Hello. Bitte. Entschuldigen.* I had no German, and I used these words nonsensically. The woman who enters, says something in what I think is German, and I say *Bitte?* And then I say *I am trapped.* Then *Nien sprechen ze Deutch*, which is very obvious. I say *I have locked myself in.*

In a very practical voice, she says, "just let me push the door in while you try it again." She pushes, and I slip the lock and I am free. "Oh, thank-you, bitte, thank-you." I wash my hands and look at my puffy eyes in the mirror. *I am trapped.*

Stewart and Diana don't seem to have noticed that I've been away for ages. Diana seems to look at me, like, *hmm. Puffy eyes. I wonder what's wrong with her.* Stewart will think I've been sulking in the toilets. I'm not the sulker in this relationship. At the beginning, when we were all at a party, my sister Julia screwed up her nose whispering over her Bacardi, *is he one of those sulky types?* I can't bear the thought that I have become a sulking woman.

∼

It is a spring day in Dover. About two minutes after we've stepped off the ferry, I realise that I've accidentally left behind the still unfinished The Brothers Karamazov. My pack is lighter, I feel lighter – as though I have shrugged away a hand on my arm trying to hold me back. Why didn't I abandon it earlier? As though I can find the person I was, before I was wailing with abandonment and clinging to my boyfriend who had stopped loving me. The brittle stone inside my gut shifts and crumbles, my chest expands.

In London, we're planning what we'll do when we fly back to Brisbane. He doesn't say, *when we're free of each other*, but I suspect that's how he feels. I feel a bit numb. We decide to stay another month and go to Scotland before we head back. On the train I am reading Thomas Hardy - all those lost connections and missed letters under the door - and I glance up over the top of the book at Stew reflected back in the train window.

I've left my brown leather jacket on the train and go to the lost property in Baker Street. Of-course I'm singing to myself, *winding your way down on Baker Street* because it is playing everywhere in London. I'm stepping more gently, more calmly. On Baker Street, I am looking at the three-story terraces with those basements below the street. These type of houses don't exist in Brisbane, and I grin to myself that I am even here, in London in spring.

I take a few more steps and another basement – this one with sparkling big windows letting you know there is a lot happening inside, catches my eye. The window of the basement carries a large circular graphic: *Wimmins' Press* and in the middle the women's liberation purple fist. In a corner of the window, in neat typeset a sign reads: *Staff Wanted. Wimmin only*. It electrified me. They have put an ad up for me on Baker Street to see. They want me. And whether it is because of Baker Street or the song or my lost leather jacket, or the spring weather, or the thought of going back to Brisbane and being alone – whatever it is, I go downstairs.

At the door I take a breath, scared to enter and nearly turn away from the big glass panelled door. Patti Smith's Horses album blares as a very tall woman with long black shiny hair opens the door as she leaves. She looks up at me, motionless on the stairs, and gives me a big grin as though she knows me.

"You should truly work there. They are great," she says to me. I never see her again but take it as a good omen. Half an hour later, I have had a cup of tea with the Scots woman editor; agreed to the wage and duties (mainly correspondence, doing first reads, and looking after diaries); and have fallen in love with Tilly, my new boss.

I want to tap dance down Baker Street. I buy cherries and gin on my way home, not worried that I found a job, but not my Italian leather jacket. I tell Stew that I've got a job at a Wimmin's Press and show him the pamphlet. Looking down at it, then sideways at me,

he is still. Holding his glass mid-air, as though he's thinking, *maybe she's a lesbian*, he says, "Today I thought of going home early. Would you stay on?"

And I find myself saying, "Yes. Yes, I'm staying."

He is catching the train to Heathrow so I just walk him to the tube. He has his pack on and we're both in such good moods – he because he's going home and me because I am at the beginning of something exciting.

At the top of the stairs he kisses me like the old days – sexually, turning up the heat. And like in the old days, I respond. I put my hands on his hips, bringing him in closer so I feel him against me. Our kiss lasts and lasts. He holds my face between his hands, "I don't know what happened. I always loved you." I'm too slow to reply, and Stew drops his hands, and moves his hips away from mine. He turns, waving and calling out, "And stay away from dodgy toilets and Dostoyevsky."

At the top of the stairs, I wonder what just happened. Not just now, but the whole damn trip.

I stay another twelve months, walking down Baker Street, not missing one day at the Wimmin's Press. I learn how to print, how to edit, how to take notes and correct copy. I wear overalls and big hoop earrings. I stop reading the 'male canon' and devour Cora Sandel and Antonia White, who our Wimmins Press rescued from obscurity. And when Margaret Thatcher is elected, I stop winding my way down at Baker Street.

My sojourn is over.

By the time I arrive home Stewart has already married.

THE END

Maria P Frino writes short stories and novels. She is a self-published author living in Sydney with her family. She writes family saga fiction, contemporary and science fiction. This is her first anthology.

Dahlia's Garden

Maria P Frino

Emily Rapson watches on as the television crew set up the lectern, add a microphone to her blazer and move things around in Dahlia's Garden. She had asked them to be careful not to disturb her mother's precious roses, and so far they have done as they were told. If this garden was disturbed in any way the crew would have the wrath of the La Perouse community to deal with. This beachside community held Dahlia's Garden in high respect, much like a famous artist's works. Emily was honoured to be doing this event today because with a degree in botany, she is more than qualified to do so.

She is here because of her mother, Dahlia. Six months ago, Dahlia succumbed to cancer but not before making a name for herself in the rose propagating, science and climate change worlds. Dahlia, a woman of fortitude, knowledge and drive was determined to help the world beat climate change by using natural means. She had succeeded in doing this with the help of scientists and botanists from London. Her dying wish was for Emily to keep this initiative alive for not only roses, but also other plant species.

Having completed the setup of *'Dahlia's Garden Foundation'*, Emily has also enlisted the expertise of the scientists and botanists Dahlia had worked with. Along with Dahlia they had begun setting up the Foundation and they too had promised Dahlia they would complete it and help Emily to run it.

"We'll be ready in ten minutes," the director tells her.

She breathes deeply to calm her nerves. This is the launch of the Foundation and Rebecca Tylen, chief scientist at The London Institute of Botanists is seated with Michelle Oscken, the best student at the Institute. On the other forty chairs are dignitaries from the local area, Emily's two good friends and Dahlia's friends and neighbours. Dahlia's front garden is the pride and joy of the La Perouse community, it is opened once a year to rose enthusiasts the world over. This house where Emily grew up is a sprawling, heritage listed Victorian-era one and Dahlia had tended to this garden with great love. Her work paid off with roses in white, dark red, sparkling yellow and pinks. When they were in full bloom, the smell of fresh roses wafted through the streets and the community was inspired by the garden's beauty.

Smiling at both her friends, Anne and Hannah, they smile back with looks of encouragement. Without them Emily would not have survived the last few years dealing with her mother's failing health and eventual death.

One of the crew is checking with Emily that she is ready because Tom Brovick, a local garden expert and member of parliament, is about to announce the beginning of proceedings. Emily takes another deep breath as she listens.

"Honoured guests…"

When Tom finishes his opening address, he announces her. Emily hears her name as if from a distance and moves in a dreamlike state towards the lectern and, standing there looking out at everyone, begins.

As she talks about the aims of the Foundation – how to fund research and find suitable species of plants, she omits one aim that is close to her heart. One day she wants a rose named after her mother – The Rapson Rose. She hasn't discussed this with other Foundation members as she needs to do more research of how roses are named. Do you have to be famous?

"... and there you have it," she says clearing her throat as emotions rise and tears prick her eyes, "The *Dahlia's Garden Foundation* is officially launched."

Placing her hand over her mouth to stem the flow of tears, she picks up her iPad and steps down. Anne and Hannah are by her side within seconds.

The caterers are buzzing around offering people champagne as well as coffee, tea and canapés. Emily has composed herself as people offer her congratulations.

"You were fine until the end. Stop worrying, everyone here understands how big this is for you," consoles Anne emptying her champagne flute.

"Yes, listen to Anne." Hannah rubs her hand gently down Emily's arm.

"I know, thanks you two. Come on, let's have some of this food the Foundation is paying for."

As they mingle with the crowd that has remained in the rose garden, Tom comes over to congratulate Emily.

"Your mother was a good friend and I miss her too. Our gardening group isn't the same without her."

How funny that he calls it a group. The La Perouse Gardening Association has over two thousand members and meets regularly. Many of the members are well-established botanists along with the enthusiastic novices.

"Thanks Tom, I appreciate you saying that. She is missed by many."

"Now, as I've said before, if there is anything you need just call, ok? Also, if you need help with anything to do with the Foundation, myself and others at the Association are at your disposal," he says placing his hand on her shoulder.

Turning her head down towards his hand not wanting to look at him, she whispers, "I appreciate you offering, I'll be in touch." She coughs trying not to be embarrassed.

As he leaves Anne and Hannah with their backs to him begin laughing. Hannah mimics his deep voice, "... I'm at your disposal. Ooh, Emily I want you."

Emily smiles despite herself. "Oh, don't gross me out. Although it was awkward when he was offering. Anyway, Hannah he's too old for me. What makes you think he wants me?"

"Oh, dear sweet Emily, are you for real? He's had his eye on you for years. Why do you think he visited your mother so often?"

"Probably because he liked her, not me. Besides, he is at least twenty years older than me."

"Like that stopped any man ever," scoffs Hannah.

The three of them laugh and then Emily excuses herself to talk to Rebecca and Michelle. "I had better do some schmoozing, the Foundation needs these two as well as Tom and his team."

She leaves them with Hannah still mimicking Tom. Shaking her head, Emily wonders whether Hannah ever takes anything seriously. She, Anne and Hannah have been friends since kindy and are inseparable. Anne, the ever efficient one of the three of them, is a marketing whizz who develops apps, and she keeps Hannah in check. Both Emily and Anne think Hannah is a frustrated comedian and should have followed that path instead of becoming a nurse. Still, her humour comes in handy with patients, many of them appreciating her making them laugh when they need it the most.

As Emily approaches Professor Rebecca Tylen and Michelle, they both smile and congratulate her on her powerful speech.

"Dahlia would be proud of you, especially when you mentioned how her work with roses has led to this point. We have our team in London already developing roses and other plants that will convert more CO_2 to help combat climate change from within nature itself."

"Thanks Professor Tylen... my mother's work is important to me"

"Call me Rebecca please, I don't like formality unless it's absolutely necessary."

"Oh yes, of course... Rebecca, I know you and my mother had

done a lot of background work, she was always a frustrated scientist. I do know she regretted not completing her studies, but she had me to consider. With Dad passing away when I was two, she didn't have a choice."

"Tragedy has a way of changing your perspective on life. Even though Dahlia wasn't fully qualified, she had the knowledge and expertise many others with degrees don't have. I don't think her becoming a full-time mother hindered her ability to learn at all."

Michelle nods in agreement, "Your mother was an inspiration to me and many other students at the Institute."

Emily thanks them both and they continue discussing the projects the Institute has planned and when she will have to travel to London.

"Now the Foundation is launched I will have more time to plan my trips. The Sydney Botanic Institute is keen to help with research as well. Professor Jones, my immediate boss has given me support and is able to travel too if needed."

"That's wonderful, we need all the support and expertise we can muster. I know of Professor Freya Jones but haven't yet had the privilege," says Rebecca

"She is keen to meet you too. And also you Michelle. She is following both your careers with interest."

"Well, we should be heading back, our plane leaves at six tonight. Again, thank you Emily for inviting us to this launch, we are excited about what is ahead of us."

Emily thanks them and sees them out the gate. She watches on as they enter the back of their hire car. Looking up she squints at the warming sun and sighs, thankful this is over. She is sure her mother is smiling down at her.

∼

Sitting at her computer, Emily looks up when Professor Freya walks in.

"I hear everything went well yesterday, you made the six o'clock news."

"Yes, and I'm glad it's over. Now I'm ready for the real work to begin."

The professor takes a seat in front of Emily. She tells her she knows there will be a lot of work, but that Emily is the best person for the job. "You know how passionate Dahlia was about preserving roses along with other plants. Climate change cannot be brushed under the carpet any longer. Things need to happen now."

Emily nods and agrees. There has been progress with climate change – sun and wind power, recycling initiatives, energy efficient products, electric cars and more. These are all technological advances and making some difference. But what the London Institute of Botanists and her workplace, the Sydney Botanic Institute, want to see is how humans can use nature to help reduce the impact of climate change. In fact, both institutes would like to see a world where this devastating environmental scourge is eradicated.

"Professor Tylen mentioned she would like you to come to London if your workload allows. I'm booking my ticket next week and I'll be arriving in London on June 30." Emily is keen for the professor to join her.

"That's a possibility, I'll look at my schedule. Now, I'll leave you to your work and again well done with the launch."

"Thanks, I appreciate that Professor."

Freya Jones is at the top of her field, she is Emily's mentor and happens to be her godmother as well. Many colleagues thought of nepotism when Emily was hired but Freya had nothing to do with Emily's appointment as Junior Botanist five years ago. In fact, she was away in America at the time and didn't know about it until she returned.

Now, as Senior Botanist and having her own team, Emily has proved her worth at this institute and she defies anyone to say otherwise.

∽

It's another sparkling day in La Perouse as the three of them sit at the kiosk with empty coffee cups in front of them. The kiosk is an affectionate name for the trendy, upbeat café, *The Bean Store*, set on the best beach in the National Park – Congwong Beach. Even though there are other cafés in the area, The Bean Store is the most popular. Run by a local family, it has been a part of La Perouse's café culture for twenty years. With its beach décor of muted blues and greens, mismatched rattan chairs and bench seating along the sides, it's a welcoming place even before you try the food.

Sitting in the booth with a view to the soft, rolling waves, they laugh at Hannah's latest joke.

"And with that, I had better get back to the hospital. I enjoy these extended lunch breaks, but I need to slow down on them, my superiors have noticed."

"Oh Hannah, with your sense of humour I'm sure you can wrangle your way out of being in trouble," says Emily.

"I wish! My humour works on the patients, not the senior nurses. See you on the weekend."

Both Emily and Anne say goodbye and then Anne orders another round of coffee after Emily agrees. "So, it's good to hear you're organised and heading to London. How nice, you'll be escaping winter for a while."

"I'm only away for ten days, but yeah, it will be nice to miss some of the winter chill. Mind you, look at today, we can't complain."

"It's autumn, it will be colder soon. Now, you were talking about some new man in your office. Come on spill."

"Nothing to tell really," answers Emily. "He's a recruit from the University of Newcastle and Freya introduced him to the team yesterday. Aaron Cumberland will be an asset because he is an expert in climate change with a degree in climate science."

"Another smart one. So, will you go out with him?"

They stop talking for a minute as their coffee is placed in front of them.

Emily continues their conversation after taking a sip. "You know the rules of staff fraternising, no, of course I won't. The institute is adamant about this rule. Break it and it means losing your job something I'm not prepared to allow to happen."

"Oh, academia and its boring rules, I'm so glad I work in the private sector. We have no rules. Besides, Marcus and I are seeing each other again."

"Really," coughs Emily then covers up her gaff with, "that's good, isn't it?" Marcus Dafoy was not her favourite person.

Anne, without a beat, continues to fill Emily in on how she is back with her ex after a break-up a few months ago. Technically they don't work together, Marcus is her client and Anne's company developed an app for him. Although Marcus is known to play around – the reason they broke up in the first place – Anne seems to think she can remove this glitch from his personality.

Emily wishes her luck with this and hopes Marcus doesn't hurt Anne again. It was Emily who helped pick up the pieces after the first time.

∼

Emily and Freya are walking out of the movie theatre. It is their monthly night out and Freya had chosen a French Film Festival for them to attend.

"Two of those movies were absolutely terrible. What was the director thinking?"

"I thought all six were good Freya, but I know the two you are talking about. Still thanks, it was nice sitting in a cinema and not having to think"

"You're nervous about the trip?"

"A little. Even though I have everything ready to take with me and I know what needs to be done, it is my first trip for the Foundation."

"You will be fine," says Freya as she hails a taxi.

Once in the taxi, they sit quietly as the driver heads to Emily's apartment first. She lives near the beach not far from her mother's house, but then nothing is far in La Perouse. Everything is within a ten-minute drive. As they drive past Dahlia's house, Emily thinks about Freya. Her mother and she had been friends since primary school and had told Emily of their trials and experiences growing up together. They had spent two years travelling and working in England and Europe, a trip that almost ended their friendship. Freya said it was too much partying and too many hot men that brought up a jealous streak in both of them. Luckily their friendship prevailed, and Dahlia didn't hesitate to have Freya as godmother once Emily was born.

When the taxi stops in front of Emily's building Freya gives her a kiss on the cheek. "If you need anything, call me. I'm sure the trip is going to go well, but I'm here if you need me."

"It would have been better if you were coming with me. Promise me you'll clear your schedule for the next one."

Freya nods, "Sure, I promise. Now scoot, I need my beauty sleep."

Emily laughs and waves back as she heads to the front entrance of her block. As the taxi fades from her view, she enters the 1940s red brick, art deco building. She loves this block and is pleased to own her apartment on the fourth floor. Her two-bedroom flat was furnished with an art deco dining table and lounge both in deep walnut courtesy of her mother's place. She walks in, flops onto the burgundy-cushioned lounge with its oversized arms and is suddenly overwhelmed with emotion because her mother's dream is happening. Does she have the energy to make the Foundation work?

The plane took off without any drama even though a storm had threatened a delay. Emily is seated and comfortable having taken her seatbelt off when allowed and had fired up her iPad. It's time to catch up on her research on a rose she would like to have named after her mother. The rose must be a hardy variety like an *iceberg* or *buff beauty*, both grow well in Australia's climate and are two of the varieties being bred to combat climate change by the Foundation. What Emily would love is a new variety, a strong variety of maybe the iceberg and buff beauty combined? This she knows is a tough call because it can take 100,000 rose crosses before a marketable rose is grown.

There are other obstacles too – did her mother do enough to be recognised? The breeder usually names the rose so will the breeders the Foundation is using allow Emily to name a successful bloom? And how long before a successful bloom becomes available? Then a committee of botanists, breeders and rose enthusiasts vote on the name. Placing her head back, Emily wonders whether this task is too huge, but she owes it to her mother and doesn't want to let it go.

Arrival at Heathrow is met with yet another storm, this time a summer one. As lightning licks the soggy sky, Emily walks off the plane and sighs, this is the start of everything her mother had worked for.

Emily can see Professor Tylen behind the group of people waiting as she walks out of the customs area. She must remember to call her Rebecca, although this will change when they're at the institute.

Rebecca is a head taller than anyone around her and her hair up in a bun adds to her height. Emily smiles as she thinks of the photos of her mother, Dahlia with Rebecca, they look like the female version of Danny DeVito and Arnold Schwarzenegger in the movie *Twins*.

"Emily, lovely to see you again. The flight was ok?"

"Thanks Rebecca. Yes, fine. Although I left a storm and found one here."

"You've caught the tail end of it, it's been an unusually warm day. Now, come on, let's get you to the hotel and then to the office."

"Yes, a shower would be good. Don't think I'll ever be used to these long-haul flights."

"I didn't realise how long it was until I visited, Australia is a long way from anywhere. Although, the little I saw I liked."

"It is beautiful, especially living near the beach as I do," says Emily as they enter the awaiting car. She is introduced to the driver by Rebecca who also tells her he will be at her disposal for her ten-day stay. Emily wasn't expecting this but is pleased not to have to worry about transport, this is only her second time in London.

The London Institute of Botanists is housed in the same building it was founded, a beautiful 1910 Edwardian building with large sash panel windows, cladding around the roofline and dark brick. The rich wooden entry door is imposing as Emily walks into the foyer. Announcing herself to the receptionist, she is asked to take a seat. The oversized leather lounge chair creaks as she sits. Emily marvels at the history exuded just in this foyer.

It's only a few minutes when Rebecca arrives along with Michelle.

"Welcome," greets Michelle, "good to see you again."

As Emily thanks her Rebecca explains that Michelle has offered to help Emily with anything she needs. "It will help her to gain further experience in this final year of study."

"How lovely, yes I welcome your help Michelle."

"I'll be around too, of course, but there will be times I won't be able to be with you, not all day anyway."

"Rebecca, thank you, I appreciate any help you are able to give me. I'm sure Michelle and I will manage."

Smiling, Rebecca says, "Follow me and I'll show you around. You have an office down from mine to use and this…" she points to a room nearest the foyer, "is where the IT department is in case you need their help."

Emily and Michelle enter the office after Rebecca bids them farewell for now, they will meet for lunch and then Rebecca will be with them for the rest of the afternoon.

"That's great, thanks. I look forward to lunch," says Emily looking around the room and feeling like she is in a scene from *Downton Abbey*. The grand windows, the adorned ceiling with ornate light shades and the oversized furniture of dark timbers and, to her delight, her desk has an inlay of green leather. It's almost sacrilege to have a computer positioned where an inkwell and elegant papers should be.

Michelle is already seated in front of the desk and going through her phone. Another anomaly in this historical room.

"Right, I guess we should start with talking to the botanists who look after the botanical garden. Would you like to show me the garden before we talk to them?"

Looking up from her phone, Michelle looks all of her eighteen years with her tortoise-shell rimmed glasses, her long, dark waves of hair pulled back in a loose ponytail and only a smattering of makeup with glossy lips. Her denim overalls over a white designer t-shirt finish her London, geek-girl vibe. Emily feels positively old at thirty in her plaid skirt and beige shirt with floral collar. Along with her black pumps, she is a tad overdressed. Even Rebecca had worn pants with sneakers and a loose-fitting shirt. Emily will tweak her wardrobe and wear something more appropriate from now on.

As they enter the garden, Emily's eyes are showered in greenery, a vibrant selection of endangered plants and trees in themed beds all leading to a conservatory where much of the research is done. This is the area Emily will spend most of her time.

"There are thousands of endangered species in this garden, all of them are being preserved and researched to save them. Obviously, you are interested in the roses, but is there anything else you wish to see?" asks Michelle.

"With the time I have I will concentrate on roses, but the Foundation will also be interested in working with your botanists on other plants that can be used to fight climate change."

"Well then, let's head to the conservatory and meet some of our botanists."

Approaching the conservatory Emily takes in a gasp, it is huge. The large glass panels are adorned with timber and decorative finials. As they walk in, the damp air attacks their noses, with both automatically placing their hands to their face.

"Welcome ladies," says a man dressed in a lab coat.

"Hi Samuel," says Michelle shaking his hand, "this is Emily Rapson from Sydney, Professor Tylen would have spoken to you about her."

"Yes. Yes, hello Emily, welcome to my humble conservatory."

Emily shakes his hand and laughs, "Humble is not a word I would describe this place, more enormous, I'd say. Nice to meet you, Samuel."

"Likewise, now what is it you need to see?"

Emily explains what the Foundation's purpose is and he asks them to follow him to the rose section. As they walk closer to the roses, their perfume mixes with the dampness to make a heady mixture of pleasant sweetness, although more potent rather than sweet.

Samuel notices Emily's face, "You'll get used to the smell, just spend a few hours a day in here."

Emily wonders whether this will happen in her short stay, but she has smelt worse things in her career. As Samuel talks, she takes in this burly man who has a pleasingly quiet voice for someone his size. Guessing he was born in London by his accent, his heritage is from somewhere in Africa.

Michelle interrupts her thoughts by saying, "Emily, we have to meet Professor Tylen for lunch. Samuel, this has been informative but maybe we can come back later?"

"Sure, I'm here all afternoon. See you then."

"Thanks for showing me your roses and I look forward to more informative talk later," says Emily turning towards Michelle but not before seeing him give her a wink.

After lunch Emily, Michelle and Rebecca are back in the conservatory chatting amongst themselves when Samuel greets them.

"Welcome once again ladies. Rebecca, how nice to see you in my humble area."

"Samuel." Rebecca answers in a clipped voice. Obviously, there is no love loss between these two.

The awkwardness disappears when Michelle asks what Samuel has in-store for them this afternoon.

"Follow me, my team is waiting for you. We have a short presentation then we will show you the progress of the plants we have been working with."

They walk behind him with Rebecca keeping her distance from Samuel. Emily wonders what has happened to cause this because from what she has seen of Samuel he doesn't seem to be that unpleasant.

As we reach the small seating area, Samuel introduces us to his team – Genevieve, Anastasia and Trevor. "This is my research team, all talented and willing to share their knowledge."

After greetings and short chats, they all sit as Trevor stands and begins the presentation.

Emily's thoughts wander between Rebecca and Samuel's strained relationship and the handsome Trevor. She decides to ask Michelle later about why Rebecca reacted to Samuel in that way, which now leaves her pondering Trevor. He's a classic Englishman – pale skin, gangly thin with a geek style, green eyes and a shock of red curls. Where Samuel is stocky and masculine, Trevor is cute in a *'I want to look after you'* kind of way. Emily laughs inwardly then tunes in to what is being said.

"So, as you have heard, we are making good progress. I'd like to thank you Emily for allowing us to access funds from your Foundation when they are available."

"Great, thanks Trevor," says Samuel standing up, "shall we go and see these plants now? Follow me."

Again, they walk behind Samuel, this time his team separates them from him. Emily looks at Rebecca who has an impassive expression, something is definitely bothering her. When Emily met Rebecca, she was an enthusiastic person, the woman behind her now is not the same person.

They walk into The Crown Arms, the local around the corner from the institute to a roar of noise. It's Friday night and the place is pumping with people catching up after work. Feeling immediately comfortable in this traditional pub with its eclectic mix of trinkets, dusty frames and congenial atmosphere, Emily smiles. With her mother's English background, she is close to Dahlia here, this feels like a home away from home. Sydney has its share of English pubs but nothing compares to the original.

"Would you like a pint?" asks Samuel.

"Sure, whatever you're having is fine, thanks."

Michelle answers too, "I'll have a Guinness, thanks."

They leave Samuel and Trevor at the bar and find a table. The rich, deep timber table, the deep burgundy clothed chairs and the reds, blacks and rich blues of the carpet all add to the comfort.

Emily is so relaxed and decides now is a good time to ask Michelle about Rebecca's reaction.

"Oh, that. Well, it's a rumour but Rebecca and Samuel had a falling out over an award he won. Apparently, he cheated with some of the criteria and when he won, Rebecca was not pleased. Don't ask me which one, I wasn't around at the time."

"If it was that long ago, why does it still worry them?"

"It's Rebecca more than Samuel. She didn't like the fact the Board dismissed her claims without an inquiry."

Emily ponders this for a minute. Rebecca is ambitious, this is obvious in how she carries out her duties, but to hold a grudge for what seems to be ten or more years seems petty.

Her thoughts are interrupted when the boys return with drinks. Making themselves comfortable, Trevor asks her questions about Australia.

"Sydney is a big city although small compared to London. I enjoy living near the beach and the weather… "

"Yeah, all that sunshine," interrupts Trevor. "One day I want to visit and surf those beaches."

"Well, I hope you do Trevor." Emily could see him riding the waves, those red curls wet and his gangly white body becoming just as red. English skin and the Australian sun don't mix. She removes this image from her mind as they keep chatting.

Many drinks later, they decide to call it a night. Samuel offers to walk Emily back to the hotel and she accepts. They chat amicably as they walk, the relaxed mood has carried throughout the night. Samuel is being a gentleman occasionally brushing her hand and sometimes walking backwards in front of her when he's making a point.

"It was my idea, this is what she wouldn't accept. How do I cheat if it's my own idea?"

He had brought up the subject of Rebecca's reaction and now I wasn't interested, it was too long ago, and Rebecca should let it go. They're colleagues and this feud is making it difficult for everyone who works with them. Emily is grateful she is only here for a short time, even Michelle hates being around the two of them. This is the reason Rebecca rarely visits the conservatory, which for a botanist is just ludicrous.

Thankfully, they arrive at her hotel and he stops talking about his issues with Rebecca. Samuel lingers and, despite herself, she asks him to join her for another drink.

Entering the Weston boutique hotel, she leads him to the small bar.

"This is quaint, isn't it?"

"Yes, and comfortable. My room is small but enough for me."

"What would you like?" asks the bartender. "By the way, we're closing the bar in fifteen minutes."

Both Emily and Samuel acknowledge her and then Samuel gives Emily a quizzical look, "So, tell me more about you. I feel like I've done nothing but talk about myself."

She smiles because he has. "I'm an only child, born in Sydney and always lived there. My parents have both passed away, my dad when I was only two. Don't remember much about him. Mum, well you know about her."

"Yes, I'm sorry. I met Dahlia a few times, she was passionate about having the Foundation up and running. We will benefit from this as Trevor mentioned earlier."

"And there's not much more to tell. You know where I work…" she stops as their drinks are placed in front of them.

"I'm sure there is a lot more to you than work," he says leaning in to kiss her.

She feels his lips on hers and tastes his boozy breath. She is sure hers is the same because she is drunk. This is the reason she was bold enough to ask him to join her here.

He picks up his drink and finishes it indicating she do the same. Picking up her gin and tonic, she gulps it down.

Samuel takes her hand and leads them to the lift, "What floor?"

"Three."

They are in the lift and he takes her kissing her mouth first, then her neck and he only stops when the lift doors open.

Fumbling for her keys with Samuel holding her from behind she leads him to her room. Throwing her bag on the floor and dropping the key, she is kissing him and pushing him towards the bed. A voice in her head is telling her to slow down but she ignores it and decides to enjoy the moment.

~

The next morning she wakes with a fierce pumping head and a mouth sour with the night's alcohol. Samuel is sleeping soundly next to her, so she creeps out of bed and heads to the bathroom.

She looks at herself in the mirror after using the toilet. Her mascara Panda eyes stare back at her. Oh, the look of shame but then she wonders why she thinks this? She had a few drinks with colleagues and then went to bed with one of them, what is so unusual? Well, the fact that Emily is a bit old-fashioned when it comes to having sex with virtual strangers. She only arrived in London two days ago and only met Samuel yesterday. What does she even know about him other than he has three brothers and two sisters?

Walking into the bathroom, Samuel uses the toilet. She hastily walks out. Now that is a reason not to sleep with someone you don't know well.

He walks out of the bathroom with a nonchalance she finds disturbing. As he moves towards her, she flinches and turns to make a tea.

"Umm, would you like tea or coffee?"

"None of that hotel rubbish for me, I'll go and get us real coffee. How do you take it?"

"No, tea is fine for me. But you go."

He dresses and heads out, "Be back. Would you like a breakfast roll or something?"

Emily would love a bacon and egg roll to soothe this hangover but declines. "Nah, I'm good." Suddenly, she doesn't want him to return. "Actually Samuel, I'm going to shower and then do some sightseeing. I'll see you on Monday, ok?"

"Oh, I was going to ask if you wanted to spend the rest of today together. How about I join you?"

"Sure...", she says not able to think of an excuse quickly enough.

"Great, then I'll pop home and change. See you in say, an hour?"

"Perfect."

She watches him leave and wonders why she feels so dirty. But then, who pees in front of someone they hardly know?

∼

Anne and Hannah are sitting at their usual booth when Emily arrives at the kiosk.

"Hey, welcome back." They say this in unison.

"Look at you looking like an English lass with your trench coat and Burberry scarf," says Hannah.

"Hi you two. Thanks, I did some shopping and doesn't my credit card know it. I couldn't resist this coat to ward off this winter chill."

"Come on, sit and order. I want all the gossip, tell us everything you did," says Anne with the enthusiasm of a friend who knows Emily did more than just work. Anne knows Emily so well she seems to have a sixth sense. How else does she know what Emily has done before she is even told?

As their brunch food arrives, Emily is half-way through telling them about how the Foundation is going to help with funds for research.

"Yes, we know what you went over to do, Emily. What we really want to know is who did you do?"

Hannah laughs and Emily feigns shock horror. "Anne, you know shy little old me doesn't shag and tell."

"Ah, then we'll force it out of you," says Hannah, "no more donuts for you until you tell."

Hannah is referring to Emily's love of cinnamon donuts, not the sickly iced ones. This is her one sweet indulgence in her otherwise healthy eating regime.

"Noooo, don't take my donuts away… alright, I'll tell you." She shows them a photo of Samuel, one she took before they went out for the Friday night drinks.

"Yummy, you did well young lady," says Anne."

"Hmm, a bit bulky for me, but he has a nice face. And look at you Emily, an African man."

"He's a good-looking man that I was attracted to, his skin colour has nothing to do with it."

"True and it's not his face that is important," laughs Anne.

Emily's face burns red despite her laughing along. Anne has always been forward when it comes to talking about sex, something Emily finds uncomfortable.

"Moving on, we went out for drinks and, well he was a gentleman and offered to walk me back to the hotel. I'd had quite a bit to drink and invited him in to have a night cap at the bar."

"An open invitation to have sex. What did you expect?"

"Like I said, Anne, I was drunk and was bolder than I usually am. We were attracted to each other and well, it was easy."

"Easy is the word," laughs Hannah, "well, come on, spill. How was he?"

Emily was again uncomfortable, and both her friends know how she feels about talking like this, but it doesn't stop them badgering her.

"Oh, come on Emily, you're an adult and allowed to have some fun. Especially when you're away."

Emily tells Anne she knows this but it's talking about it that makes her squirm. "Besides, we only did it the once. After he peed while I was still in the bathroom the morning after, I… well, I was repulsed. Who pees in front of someone they hardly know?"

"Oh, please Emily, you just had sex with the guy. He was obviously comfortable being around you."

"Hannah, that doesn't change how I feel about what happened. Things became uncomfortable even though he offered to come sightseeing with me. Which he did."

"I'm sure he wanted more of you after sightseeing, right?"

"Yes Anne, but I told him I had a headache and felt some jet lag. The headache part was true, I was still hungover."

"The good old headache excuse. Mind you the jet lag would have been enough."

"I feel it when I come home, it wasn't a problem over there. Anyway, we had some uncomfortable times in the office and conservatory. He even tried to ask me what was wrong, but I was able to change the subject, or we were interrupted. In the end, he stopped asking."

"Well, that's so boring. Emily you could have had more fun with him. Honestly, he was obviously comfortable with you."

"Anne, give it a break. I couldn't get past what he did, and yes, I did enjoy the night with him, that will be a nice memory. Now, tell me what you two have been up to while I was gone."

Hannah says, "Not much for me to tell. Same old same old for me, but Anne has some news."

Emily looks at Anne expectantly.

"I caught Marcus again. This time with an eighteen-year-old and we'd only been back together for a month. We're over for good now."

Emily places her arm over Anne's shoulder, "Oh, I'm so sorry." She wasn't at all sorry but didn't let on. "Where did you catch him this time?"

"At Pepe's Pizza. He was nuzzling her neck in front of everyone. I had gone to collect my takeaway. And, disgustingly, he tried to tell me she was just a friend."

Hannah smirks, "That's so Marcus. You're better off without him, Anne. You deserve better."

"I do don't I? No more bad boys for me."

Both Hannah and Emily laugh because they know Anne can't help herself when it comes to picking men who are wrong for her.

She is with Freya at a restaurant in The Rocks, the historical area of Sydney. They had spoken at work about her trip and Freya was pleased with the amount of information Emily had brought back with her. Freya knew the Foundation was going to be a bonus for both institutes.

"And then we went for a drink, but Rebecca didn't join us." Emily completes telling her godmother about the Friday night excluding the part with Samuel. She doesn't need to know about Emily's love escapades, the few she does have.

"I'm glad you were able to relax, and it wasn't all work for you. They are a good bunch with a lot of experience between them. This project will certainly help put a dent in climate change, at least that is the aim anyway."

The Thai food they ordered is placed in front of them and they eat as they continue talking about Emily's trip.

"You enjoyed the shopping then? How good is Oxford Street? All those shops all in a row. What about Westfield, did you have a chance to visit one?"

"No, but I also thought why visit a Westfield in London. Wouldn't it be similar to ours here? Anyway, I ran out of time, I only shopped once."

"Probably, with a few added European stores."

"I spent time with Rebecca and Michelle on the second weekend. Rebecca drove us to Bath and we stayed the night. It was glorious – the drive, the company and discovering historic Bath."

"How lovely. I'm glad you had a good time, you seemed worried before you left."

Emily remembers how nervous she had been, but it was more about what she would be expected to do rather than the socialising. "It's Mum's legacy and I didn't want to stuff up. The social side was easy, it was the work involved that concerned me."

"You did well, so no need to worry next time."

"You'll be with me next time, I hope."

"We'll see. Yum, this laksa is delicious," says Freya changing the subject.

Emily asks Freya what she thinks about a rose being named after her mother.

"A brilliant idea. Do you have a rose in mind?"

"I like *Buff Beauty* and *Iceberg*, but I haven't decided yet. I'm still researching the idea. Both these roses are hardy and do well in Australia. Maybe a combination of the two?"

"Both are lovely roses. So, you're thinking of a rose that will counteract climate change? Is that what you mean by combining the two?"

"Yes, it's something I'd have to look into with a breeder. I like the idea of her having a rose named after her that does what she worked so hard to promote."

Freya smiles placing her hand on Emily's, "That is a beautiful thought and one you should pursue."

∼

Her mobile buzzes. She looks at it with bleary eyes, it five in the morning and Hannah is calling her. What?

"Hello."

"Emily, I'm so sorry to call you but…" Hannah clears her throat. "Freya has been brought to the hospital; she's had a heart attack."

"What? No, I was with her last night. She was fine." Emily is frozen, sitting up in bed like a puppet. Someone is pulling at strings to keep her up.

"You need to come in, she's asking for you."

"How… how bad is she?" asks Emily, the words catching in her mouth.

"She's conscious, which is good, but you need to get here asap."

"Ok, I'll be there as soon as I can. Keep her alive Hannah, I don't want to lose her too." This thought shakes her to the core and her mother's face, a loving face, is in front of her. It's almost as if she is giving Emily the strength she needs.

Arriving at St Margaret's on Oxford Street, Emily rushes to emergency where Hannah had told her to go. Hannah is there to meet her as she falls into her friend's arms sobbing.

"She's stable now. Come on, she wants to see you."

Freya is in a cubicle with only those paper-like curtains separating her from the next patient. Emily sees a pallid woman with wrinkles that weren't there last night. Her eyes are sockets and she is barely breathing.

"Freya, oh…" Again, Emily breaks down and has to compose herself as Freya is trying to tell her something.

"I'm going to be… fi…" Freya whispers followed by a shallow cough, "doctors know what to do."

"Of course, you are. I won't let you leave me."

Hannah comes over and asks Emily to speak with the doctor. "This is Dr Hamish, he's been looking after your godmother for some time."

"What do you mean? How long has she been here?"

"Hello, Emily. What Hannah means is, I've looked after Freya since she presented with severe angina five years ago. I'll be managing her condition at this hospital as well, she'll be here for at least ten days."

"Right, umm, I didn't know. She never told me. Sorry, this is such a shock." Emily knows how private Freya is and this is probably the reason why she didn't divulge this illness to her. Still, she is angry with her now but tries to stay calm because Freya needs her help not her anger.

"I understand this is a shock to you, but Freya came in early enough for us to control things…"

Emily interrupts him, "What? She came in on her own. She could have called me."

"It's ok, Freya had the sense to call triple zero. She came in by ambulance and this is what has saved her."

Emily tries to answer but can't piece her words together. The doctor asks Hannah to look after Emily while he checks on Freya.

"Come with me, I'll take you to the cafeteria. Are you hungry?"

The last thing on Emily's mind is food. "No, strong coffee." Again, words her won't come out.

"You're in shock Emily, but Dr Hamish is a good cardiologist, he'll fix Freya's heart and she'll be home soon."

"She needs surgery?"

"Yes, but Dr Hamish will explain all this to you. I'm sorry I had to ring you with bad news."

"Don't apologise, I'm glad I was back home, this could have happened while I was in London. That would have been so much worse."

"I guess so."

Before Hannah could say anything further, they were called back to emergency, Dr Hamish needed to speak to Emily.

Sitting in her office, Emily is thinking about the last two weeks. Freya survived the heart attack. Dr Hamish was adamant she takes it easy and was not to return to work for three months. Freya had not been pleased but Emily promised the doctor she would make sure Freya looked after herself because Emily was going to make sure of it.

She opens her personal laptop and starts researching naming roses. Having spoken with Freya about using the Foundation as a reason to name a rose after Dahlia, Freya had said to use everything at her disposal and to include all the good work her mother had done. The hard part was going to find someone who will breed a new rose for her. Emily had decided to name a hybrid rose after her mother, one that is hardy and will combat climate change. This was Dahlia's legacy and the reason for the Foundation. She opened several tabs and bookmarked them for later because right now she had a meeting to go to.

Entering the boardroom, she sits next to Aaron. He smiles and his white teeth glow in the semi-lit room. She is sure he has had them whitened because he drinks coffee like it is water.

"How's Professor Jones doing?"

It takes Emily a moment to realise he is asking about Freya, she rarely thinks of her by her professional name. "Oh, she's resting and doing ok. Thanks for asking."

"That's good to hear. Listen, I was wondering, would you like some help with the Foundation? I can help with preparations for your next trip if you like?"

"Aaron, that would be great, thanks. How about we talk about it after this meeting?"

"Sounds good."

They both turn towards the white board as one of the professors starts the meeting.

∾

Muffled classical music hums from behind the door as Emily raps her hand on it. No response. Obviously, Freya can't hear because of the music. Emily had already tried the doorbell knowing Freya had not had it fixed, but it's an automatic reaction. She smiles as she remembers when Freya had this novelty doorbell installed, a dog barking, and how scared she was as a child to press it. This was something out of character for Freya, who was polite and nice to everyone.

"It keeps unwanted jerks away. Besides, I like the idea I'm being protected by a dog."

"But you don't have a dog?" Emily had said with the innocence of a child.

"No, but people think I do and that keeps me safe."

Emily had not understood until she was in her teens and the doorbell had scared a thief. Unfortunately, Freya's neighbour was robbed instead.

Knocking harder after her mind came back to the present, she waited a few minutes but again, nothing. Panic creeped up her spine. *Oh no, what if she's had another attack?*

"Freya," she screams knocking harder still. "FREYA!"

The music stops and Emily's heart begins to settle as the door creaks open.

"You don't have to yell, I was in the backroom with the door closed."

"Oh sorry," Emily gulps, "you had me worried."

"I'm fine. Come in, I'll get you a drink."

Emily is pleased to see Freya's colour come back into her face. She has lost weight, but her appetite is better so at least she is eating full meals again.

They settle on the lounge as Freya tells Emily she has listened to the doctor and rested. "It's only been a few weeks and I'm missing work, but I've started painting again. I cleaned up the back room and it's now my studio. It's warmer than the garage in winter and not such a hothouse in summer."

"Why didn't you call me? I would have helped you clean the room."

"Stop fretting, I did it over a few days. Like I said, I'm listening to Dr Hamish."

Emily calms down and begins telling Freya about her research. Surprisingly, it's not expensive to have a rose named after a loved one and many breeders have lovely unnamed roses on their websites. "The problem is none of these unnamed roses can help with climate change. So, my challenge is to find a breeder who will develop a hybrid."

"How is that a problem? What about the institute in London?"

"I had thought of them, Freya, but the ones they are working on are still experimental."

"We know it takes years to develop roses, and any plant for that matter, to alter the UV pigments and help with the natural fight against climate change. The institute has a head start with this so I think you should approach them first."

Emily thinks about this and the thought of having to speak with Samuel again often doesn't thrill her.

"Speak to Rebecca, she'll have the staff in the conservatory work on one for you."

"That's a good idea, I'll bring it up with her on my next trip. You know that is only a month away, are you ok for me to go?"

"Emily, please, I can look after myself."

"I've asked Hannah and Anne to pop in on you when I'm away, it will ease my mind."

"If that makes you feel better, then fine. You know I love both of your friends."

Relaxing into the lounge, Emily sips on her tea and listens to Freya as she talks about her plans to incorporate more exercise into her routine to keep her heart healthy. Emily feels lucky to have her sitting here, and healthier than a few weeks ago because she thought she was going to find her dead on that awful drive to the hospital.

"These are for you," says Emily handing Hannah a posy of pink roses.

"Lovely, thanks. What are these for?"

"A thank you for looking after Freya."

"Emily, that's my job."

"I know Hannah, but it was great for Freya to have someone she knows caring for her, I think it helped with her recovery."

"Maybe. Oh, these have a soft smell, thanks again."

They hug each other and sit back on the bench seat waiting for Anne who had texted Emily saying she would be late.

The kiosk is full as it usually is on a Saturday morning. The queue outside is growing as people wait for their brunch orders or to have a table.

"Hello, my lovelies, sorry I'm late." Anne bounces in wearing her gym gear, her tights a shiny metallic red. She certainly makes an entrance.

"What happened, did you do a later class."

"No, Emily, one of the instructors was leaving to have a baby and we had a farewell for her. I've already had coffee; you guys go ahead and order. Didn't I say that in the text?"

She hadn't but that is Anne, always in a hurry and forgetting details.

"I'll go and order. The usual Emily?"

"Thanks Hannah."

"Nice roses."

"I gave them to Hannah as a thank you for looking after Freya."

"Oh yes, I'm sorry, how is she doing?"

"Fine. I was there yesterday after work and she has set up her studio in the backroom. She told me she's listening to the doctor, which eases my mind."

"Good to hear. It was a shock."

Emily nods as Hannah returns to the table and Emily reminds them about looking out for Freya when she's in London. Both her friends tell her not to worry, they will make sure her godmother is well looked after.

Back in her office after the meeting, Aaron is sitting opposite her detailing his plans for greater use of his climate science degree for both the Institute and the Foundation.

"That's a generous use of your skills, Aaron. Have you discussed this with anyone else?"

"I have and the Board has agreed in general, Professor Jones has signed off on it and I'm willing to put in the work."

Emily is impressed by him and his ambition. He sits comfortably in the old office chair and his lab coat is impeccably white, crisp even. She has also watched his progress since he started, he is an amiable person, and the rest of the staff have high praise for him. As he talks, Emily takes in his personable nature. His dark eyes show passion, his square jaw juts out making him look older than his twenty-eight years. She notices he has a slight chin dimple, she hadn't seen that before. Possibly because they have not spent this long together since he started.

"Well, I've taken up a lot of your time, I must get going."

He snaps her out of her reverie. "This has been enlightening, thanks for telling me about your plan," she says lifting herself out of her chair to shake his hand.

"Thank you," he says taking her hand and shaking it firmly, "I'm glad you're on board too."

She looks directly at him realising she had not actually said that, but as their look lingers, she decides she is onboard with it.

"Um, by the way, would you like to go out for a drink some time?"

Emily stops for a minute wondering whether she should. "Yes, that would be nice, thanks." So much for the institute rules, but she can't see a problem with one date.

The drink date became a lunch date, and a pleasant one at that. Aaron had come past her office and they went to lunch at The Rocks. The Albert Arms was full of young professionals on this Friday, and Aaron fitted in well in his designer rolled-up jeans, brown casuals and dark blue linen shirt. Casual Fridays is still going strong. They ordered and went to the outside tables all adorned with umbrellas and tin cutlery holders. Music sounds from the speakers above them, chilled out tunes not too loud to drown out their conversation.

Aaron spoke of his family in Newcastle and how he was close to his brothers. He is the youngest so was always looked after by his older two. "Jeff and David both live in Newcastle, are married and have two kids each. Dad passed away two years ago, so Mum sees my brothers and the grandkids regularly. This keeps her going."

"I'm sorry to hear about your dad, I lost my mother two years ago too."

"Yes, I know. She started the Foundation you're now a part of."

They continue talking as their food is placed in front of them. Aaron tells her of his love of music and how he plays guitar. "It soothes me to play and helps ease my anxiety."

"You're anxious, that's a surprise, you seem calm to me."

"I keep it under wraps as I have learned how to deal with it. Learning to play has helped with this."

Emily feels a mothering concern for him wanting to soothe that anxiety. She listens as he keeps talking, his good looks belie what he is saying about the anxiety that has clouded his life.

Later in the evening Emily is with Anne and Hannah at the same pub.

"So, how was lunch with your hunky colleague?"

"Hunky? You haven't even met him, Anne."

"From what you've told us, that's how I picture him. Or maybe I have it wrong, do hunks have dimples on their chins?"

"Possibly," chimes in Hannah, "whatever, he sounds nice."

"He is nice, and when he told me about being anxious, well now I just want to look after him."

"Oh Emily, you have such a caring nature. So, when are you seeing him again?"

"He wants some help with shopping tomorrow, not that he needs it, he dresses well for a scientist."

"What, no dorky oversized pants and shapeless blazers?"

"Ha, no Hannah. He has a style I like. Oops, did I say that out loud?"

"So much for the rules about not dating someone you work with, Emily," says Anne with a smirk.

"Yeah, well, screw the rules. I like him so I'm going to keep seeing him if that's what he wants too."

∽

Emily is holding the plaque with Dahlia's photo and the rose named in her honour – The Rapson Rose. The London Institute of Botanists had come through with a hybrid rose within two years, a record time. This was made possible with funds from the Foundation and Samuel, along with his team, had pushed through the breeding with a few different types of roses to select this final one. The Rapson Rose is a pale pink one with a white centre that is exposed as it blooms.

She is on zoom thanking the team in London. "You have blown me away with how quickly this has happened and have honoured both myself and my mother."

"You are welcome, Emily and I'm sure your mother will be happy with this rose too," says Rebecca.

Samuel chimes in, "With the funds we were able to concentrate on this hybrid, I'm happy for you Emily."

"Thanks Samuel, it means a lot to me the efforts you and your team have placed in this project." She and Samuel had restored their friendship when she returned to London for her second trip, she counted him as one of her good friends now.

"Also, congratulations to you and Aaron, I hear you're pregnant."

"We are Samuel, thanks. The baby is due next March."

There are cheers and well wishes from everyone on zoom with Michelle adding her congratulations.

"That's wonderful news, Emily. I look forward to seeing you and Aaron with the baby in London."

"Thanks Michelle, I hope we can all visit one day. Thank you all again for a fabulous effort, now I say goodbye until next time. Thanks for your time."

She hears them all say goodbye to her as they all sign off and Rebecca is the only one remaining on the chat. "Thanks for everything Rebecca, I could not have done this without you."

"You're welcome, Emily. Look after yourself and I look forward to meeting your baby soon too. Goodbye." Rebecca signs off too.

Emily stands and places her hand on her small bump. A tear falls as she wishes her mother was here to witness everything that has happened.

THE END

Adelaide Hunter lives in Sydney. She works with sound waves during the day and writes under the cover of darkness with ink, at night. She is a fan of perceptions, boundaries and meeting places - tangible and intangible. Adelaide is curious as to how these affect relationships between persons past, present and future. This is her first anthology.

The Dig

Adelaide Hunter

She felt it coming. A wave of unease swept over Pip as the wind changed direction, causing her to shiver. Her aunt would have said, "there are ghosts circling your grave."

The swirling of dust around her worn leather boots continued for a few minutes, then subsided. It was never a good sign. She looked away from the excavation site at Ephesus to gaze upon the blue-green Aegean Sea and took a deep breath in, the tang of salt tingling her nostrils.

Stretching her thin arms and shaking out the stress of a long week, she dreamed of being back on the boat listening to the gentle lap-lap of the water against the hull. Sometimes she wished she could disappear and reinvent herself, just to escape the maddening world and step off the treadmill for a while.

This trip was the last of its kind for Dr Pip Dunbar. She reflected on her work over thirty years in the Middle East, Africa, Poland, Russia, Egypt and now, Ephesus. Having a PhD in history - specialising in myths and rituals - and working as a documentary photographer, was a winning combination and opened many doors for her.

History and photography fed each other and brought originality and depth to her research. It was a niche specialty, and she was in demand. Now she wanted time to indulge her interests in painting and writing, and wherever that led her.

She felt a certain freedom beckoning, and laughed to herself, remembering the cruise around the Greek islands that she had taken, before alighting at the last stop - Ephesus, to join the dig.

The rather attractive captain of that ship, as was custom, had invited a selection of the guests to join him at the Captain's table for dinner on the last evening. Pip was one of the invited. It was a strange night because her name-tag read 'Hannah Richards' due to some confusion on the part of an apprentice crew member. She decided to play along with being Hannah and enjoyed the entire evening. There was a certain freedom to being somebody else, and she relished it.

As she was the only person alighting at Ephesus, the discussion turned to the history and beliefs of the people who lived there thousands of years ago. One of the guests - an elderly woman named Sarah, who wore a loosely woven, deep indigo coloured wrap - provided some information about the gods of the time.

"Artemis was the main goddess worshipped. She was somewhat of a paradox, being the guardian and helper of women in childbirth, but sometimes her arrows ended their lives suddenly."

"Is she the goddess depicted with a bow and arrow?" Pip asked.

"Yes, in mainland Greece she is, but in Ephesus, she is revered as a fertility goddess and is often seen with many breasts or bulls testes displayed across her chest." This information provided some good-natured banter around the table as Sarah continued.

"The Ephesians even built a temple to Artemis, but now, only the foundations are left. The best of the ruins are kept in the British Museum. Still, it would be worth visiting the foundations if you have time," she said, directing her advice to Pip.

"But a warning - even to this day, there is a sect still worshipping Artemis in these parts. And they believe that she has power over events and will reward those who are loyal to her and punish those who are not. So be good!" Sarah said with a smile, and reached for her wine.

This caused a rumble of discussion and a couple of locals related various anecdotes from stories they heard as children. Once or twice during the dinner, the captain held Pip's gaze for slightly longer than was comfortable. Was he flirting with her?

"Doctor, come on over and take a look at this," shouted Delvin Sapsford, waving his hat to attract her attention. Pip twitched, startled by the interruption to her reverie, and turned back to find a yellow spotted bowtie bobbing up and down in the distance. It was attached to an odd little man, jumping up and down like a leprechaun. Closing her eyes, she breathed deeply and savoured the image of the sea, and thoughts of the captain for a moment longer, before returning to reality.

She bent over and hauled her photographic kit onto her shoulder, adjusted her weather-beaten hat and trudged across the dry dirt of centuries to the growing number of people gathering around Sapsford. She nodded at the man, who was leaning on his pickaxe and chewing a wad of gum, and knelt down to see what the fuss was about. The hole that the pickaxe created caused a shaft of light to pierce the ground into what she suspected was a cavernous space beneath. She pulled her telescopic camera from her kit and fed it carefully into the small hole in the ground. It was important to disrupt as little as possible.

She looked at the screen on her phone, where the images from the camera beneath the soil were transmitted. Light with dust particles suspended in ancient time, swirled about like magic on the screen. Pip steered the scope inside the space until the camera pointed at something recognisable. A bright image appeared on the screen, and Pip froze.

Magnificent coloured frescoes - red, blue and gold, painted on the walls of the space below, stared back at her. Perhaps it was a palace or a synagogue, she mused. She had seen nothing like it at any of the sites she had worked over the years. Pip blinked a few times, moved the scope around carefully, and looked again. This time she saw dolphins frolicking in the sea, servants carrying bowls of fruit and people resting on their sides at what looked like a banquet. She was looking back through time at a pristine space untouched by humans for centuries. Now she understood. She released the breath that had been captive in her lungs and stood up.

"Well?" asked Sapsford, moving his weight from one foot to the other.

"I'm pretty certain these frescoes are the ones described in the parchment we unearthed," said Pip. "As that was dated around the same time as the Dead Sea Scrolls, this site is far more ancient. I think it's some kind of antechamber that leads to somewhere much grander."

A moment of stunned silence before excited chatter and smiles all around the group followed. The workers hurriedly beckoned other members of the dig to come over. Like buzzards around a carcass, they gathered as every single person at that site knew they would share in the substantial prize gifted by the Smithsonian Trust. This find would make the historic journals, archaeological archives and possibly even the New York Times. Daisy Sapsford, wife of Delvin, and journalist documenting the dig, was already sharpening her pencil for the press release. Each harboured secret dreams of success and the accompanying fanfare.

For some, it meant a simple foot in the door on other digs in exotic locations around the world. The more academically minded, imagined papers being accepted and cited in respected journals, and the coveted invitation to speak at any number of international conferences. A book deal or podcast series was in the minds of a few. Pip could almost hear their thoughts.

Delvin dropped his pickaxe and, stepping closer, nudged Pip aside, grabbed the scope and Pip's phone and looked for himself.

"Well, I'll be a monkey's uncle! It's amazin' - the colours!"

Pip frowned. She'd seen it too many times before and wondered how long it would take for the greed and ambition to manifest. Not long, it seemed. Fortunately, she had made no friends on this dig. She learned the hard way not to do that. Pip turned to address the workers and held up both hands in an effort to quell their noise.

"This is truly a wonderful but unexpected finding. We need to research the exact customs and beliefs of the people of this period so that we can understand more. It's my strong recommendation to halt excavation and leave the site untouched. The research needs to be evaluated, and then a decision on how to proceed can follow," she said, noting the grumbled murmurs and shuffling feet of the workers.

"Why thank you, Pip dear," said Delvin in his long Texan drawl, "but as the director of this dig, I'm invitin' y'all to a shindig this evening at the Big House. Pardon the pun! For now, we will continue to excavate as there is much to discover and we're burnin' daylight here." Cheers from the workers hammered on Pip's eardrums and she took a small step backwards.

Pip looked down at the short Texan with the yellow spotted bowtie and wondered how he came to be in charge of this dig. But she knew why deep down. The man was a yes-man, and that's what the wealthy sponsors wanted. Results at any cost. The workers were happy too. They wanted to share the prize-money, the fame and the honour, but mostly the money. Who cared about the customs and beliefs of a people long dead? Life was for the living.

"Well, Mr Sapsford, you'll excuse me then. I'm done." Pip turned away from the group, packed up her gear and walked to the shore. She would talk her way onto the next cruise ship at port and stay for the rest of the scheduled journey. After all, her time was her own and there was so much to explore. She could be anybody now. And she didn't look back.

~

Later that evening, Pip sipped ouzo at the bar on a much grander cruise ship than the previous one she had travelled on. The cruise was organised by a British company and the crew was mainly British.

She was fortunate enough to join the ship after an elderly couple had cancelled their trip at the last minute. Refreshed after a long hot shower, she felt the unease of the day melt away as the ship made its way around the Greek Islands. It was after her second ouzo that she heard the news over the radio and wondered if perhaps she'd indulged a little too enthusiastically in the local spirits.

"This is Trish Goodwin with the BBC news," the polished female voice announced over the crackly airwaves.

"A terrible tragedy occurred at 7.30pm local time in Ephesus, Turkey. A large house known as 'The Big House' located on the outskirts of Ephesus and mainly used as tourist accommodation, disappeared when the ground underneath the house subsided. We are crossing live to our reporter Roland Butterfield, at the site now. Can you tell us what you know, Roland?"

"Good evening Trish. The scene here is one of complete devastation in what can only be described as a freak occurrence. All that remains is an enormous black hole in the ground. Under the floodlights, nothing can be seen, although rescuers are still searching for survivors. As far as the authorities know, it's believed there were twenty-two people staying at The Big House. These were a team of archaeologists and assistants, working at an excavation in the centre of Ephesus. To date, there are no reported survivors of that team. All were believed to be present, due to a celebration that was taking place at the house this evening, according to locals. Tragically, they are all now missing, and so far, there is no sign of life."

"Is there anything at all left behind?" Trish asked.

"The jaws of the sinkhole swallowed everything Trish, except for a yellow spotted bowtie. If there are any members of that archaeological team listening to this broadcast, please contact the authorities immediately." Roland paused to catch his breath amidst the dust, then took a sip of water.

"Fortunately, the famous ruins of Ephesus remain intact." He coughed before clearing his throat.

"Roland Butterfield, BBC news, Ephesus, Turkey."

In the temple's antechamber beneath the earth, at the site of the dig - for it was a temple and not a palace or a synagogue—the ghosts of Ephesian royalty gathered. Spirits of the kings and queens of old, circled the tomb in the middle of the space. For the antechamber housed the tomb of their Queen - she who was secret from recorded history. As the spirits assembled around Queen Alexandra's final resting place, they toasted her and each other, waiting for her spirit to return home to her body. It was essential for her body to remain intact and hidden so she could rise again at the preordained time. For the ghosts knew that their Queen was the beloved human sister of the Goddess Artemis and was protected by her.

And true to the warning that Sarah gave Pip, Artemis bestowed certain favours on those who were loyal, and ruthlessly punished those who were not. Delvin Sapsford knew that now. The hole that the pick-axe created on the surface of the ground above, became smaller and smaller until it was no more. Queen Alexandra was safe again.

Pip Dunbar ordered her third ouzo and offered a silent toast to lost friends, lost colleagues and lost loves. She thought about contacting the authorities but didn't have the strength for that now. Her guilt at surviving was like a lead weight within her heart. All those people – simply vanished. Should she, the twenty-second soul, be with the twenty-one others?

"May I interrupt your thoughts?" asked a deep voice beside her.

Pip flinched and glanced up to see the owner of the voice. She blinked then abruptly looked down to study the contents of her glass, moving it between her fingers, while she scrambled for words. The deep voice in the uniform belonged to the same man at the

Captain's dinner on the earlier cruise-ship. In fact, it was the captain himself.

"Let's start again," he said, with a hint of merriment that betrayed his authority.

"I'm John. John Prendergast. And I remember your name."

Pip opened her mouth and paused, before turning to face him. "Hannah," he said, "Hannah Richards."

Pip smiled as they clinked their glasses. Life is good, she thought. "Santé!"

THE END

Joanna Makris is curious, funny, and believes laughter is the way to happiness. She loves creativity and expression in all forms, and enjoys working with technology, spirituality and breathing life into new ideas. New to the world of writing, she has settled on fiction, using her dry wit to encourage a giggle or two.

Confessions

Joanna Makris

"Just put it in! What's taking so long?"

My face was flushed, and beads of sweat were forming above my upper lip.

Matt was digging away furiously. His jeans, slightly loose from excessive physical exertion, were sliding downwards. His butt had been peering at me just above his jeans, but was now edging its way out, as if trying to pass me a secret message. A message I didn't want to see.

He stood up and shuffled over, tugging at his jeans along the way.

"Can you do a better job of digging up a hole with your hands? This I gotta see!" he mumbled. "You're still sitting on the ground!"

I stared at the buckle on his belt, and a few stray pubic hairs waving at me. On impulse, I was about to wave back, unable to think of anything practical to say, but thought better of it. "You might want to take your belt in a notch," I said to his buckle, admiring the engraving around its edges.

After sizing up the small cradle of dirt Matt had formed, my gaze fell onto the heavy object in my arms. How could this religious work of art, a solid gold statue of St George adorned with precious gems, be crammed into a dent in the ground? Its gems reflected light in all directions, so much so, that I was afraid it would spark the neighbour's attention.

"Hold this for a second," I said.

"Shit, this is heavy!" he wheezed. "How did you carry it to your car?"

"I hobbled."

We both looked down at this weighted, valuable object, incongruously out of place in my petite garden with its laughing miniature gnomes.

How did I get myself into this? How, in a matter of weeks, did my life digress from a straight path into a labyrinth?

Three weeks before, I planned a visit to my Aunt Clelia. She was my father's sister, an energetic woman in her early 60s, who lived about a 3-hour drive away from the city.

I hadn't seen her in nearly two years, since the day of my father's funeral, mostly because I don't enjoy travelling long distances by car. I usually develop severe hunger pangs along the way, and end up severely bloated from devouring mountains of salty crisps.

She'd sounded surprised when I called to announce my upcoming visit.

"Oh my, I haven't heard from you in a while," she'd remarked in a suspicious tone.

She'd never really approved of me, and I peppered the conversation with comments about family love, hoping she'd lower her guard.

Keeping the true purpose of the trip to myself, I grabbed some salty snacks, and left for my aunt's house.

My aunt lived on the edge of the town, in a country heritage house with a green picket fence. She'd been living there for years, claiming that the feng shui of that spot was ideal, and believed it had contributed to her good fortune. I parked in her driveway and pushed the empty crisps bags under the seat, counting them as I packed each one away.

"Hello, my dear! How are you?" Aunt Clelia stepped out into her garden to greet me. "You're looking a little heavier?" she continued, her eagle eye measuring the width of my hips. It wasn't difficult for her to do that, as her short, wiry frame peaked somewhere near my shoulders, and her dark, close-set eyes were on a level with my chest.

"Come in, come in!" she guided me into her living room, pushing my lower back so that my stomach led the way.

I sat down on her velvet couch, then thought better of it and placed myself on a wicker chair. She smiled her approval before darting into the kitchen.

My aunt's living room was a display of ornaments and wealth, and she cared for both with precision. She was a woman who took pride in her possessions, and her fortune was due to amassing valuable objects that had come her way either by inheritance, purchases, or through the art of gentle persuasion.

"I baked a scrumptious orange cake. Will you have some?" she ordered, returning from the kitchen.

"Oh, thanks," I replied, taking a piece of the fluffy dessert.

"So, how are you? How is work?" she asked.

"Busy, quite busy. I've taken on a managerial role and have a team of three under me. But the hours are long, and my laptop is my constant companion."

"My dear, that's wonderful. Just be careful your constant companion doesn't replace a real one," she remarked.

I let that comment pass and munched into the moist cake, dropping a few crumbs onto her newly polished floor. My aunt's beady eyes didn't miss a speck.

"I'm so sorry!" Mortified, I began wiping the floor with a paper towel, dropping the rest of my crumbs in the process. I continued wiping, watching the smear I had created expanding, creeping in circular motions towards my aunt's feet.

"No, no!" she cried. "You're dirtying the floor! I'll do it later. Come, we'll go out into the garden," she continued, in an effort to get me away from the interior of her home.

Having minimal baking skills, I mused on why butter was used as a cake ingredient, when cleaning it was obviously a nightmare.

We stepped out into the back garden, descending a narrow staircase, and I picked a flower from the pretty pink bougainvillaea growing near the last few steps.

"What happened to that flower?" My aunt glared at me.

I gawked at her, mouth agape. "I.. um, it was about to fall off?"

She walked past me with a haughty tilt of her head, strutting into the middle of the garden.

Regaining my focus, I glided up to my aunt and said in a low voice, "Auntie, do you remember, by chance… My father had a piece of artwork, a solid gold statue of St George. Do you know what happened to that?"

She was studying the mildew on her rosebush, when she whirled around to face me, pulling a roseleaf from its stem.

"What? That old thing! What made you bring that up?" she snapped, her eyes aflame.

Snatches of conversation about this valuable piece flashed through my mind, conversations between my father and my aunt, when a shrill sound interrupted my memories.

"Mum!" yelled a high-pitched voice from my aunt's kitchen.

"Your cousin is here. Come and say hello," my aunt retorted.

The cousin she was referring to was Jake, her youngest son, who still lived with her. A 27-year-old mama's boy, he made no decision without his mother's advice.

"You've got to go to the shop with me! I can't decide which phone to buy," he whined. "I want to go now!"

Jake appeared at the kitchen window, and on spotting me in the garden, squinted in an attempt to recognise me.

"You remember your cousin from the city, don't you?" Aunt Clelia asked him. "The one with the salt addiction."

93

"Oh, yeah," replied Jake, a silly grin replacing his earlier squint. He giggled a sly, girly laugh and replaced it with a frown.

"Mum! Let's go, I really need a phone!" he moaned.

My aunt threw me a nervous glance and said, "Wait here, I won't be long," before whisking her son away in the direction of the local mall.

Clelia's priority was her son's shopping spree, and her bizarre reaction in the garden had dampened any hopes I had of gaining any information.

It was getting hot, and my bulky jacket was cumbersome. I also needed to use the bathroom. It was at the bottom of a hallway lined with firmly closed doors, and as I proceeded down the hallway, I stopped in front of a door that was slightly ajar. It was the door to my aunt's bedroom, and cocking my head to one side, I spotted a brown vintage trunk in the corner of the room.

I tiptoed, for no apparent reason, into the room, as only a family of dolls was there to greet me. The trunk coaxed me on, and I fiddled with its latch, but it was tightly sealed.

Aunt Clelia owned a tiny music box. She'd had it since she was a young girl. It had a delicate ballerina perched on top, and as a child, she'd use the music box to stash away treasures and trinkets. It was on top of her book stand, and on opening it, I found three keys within the silk lining.

None of them seemed to work, as I poked each key into the vertical keyhole. I tried them again, accidentally inserting a key upside down, and heard the latch open with a click.

And there it was: my father's statue. It was resting on a piece of blue fabric, almost casually, as if it was an item of no importance. I peeked out of the window. No one in sight, and without a second thought, I removed the valuable artwork, locked the trunk and returned the key to the music box.

Glad I was wearing my bulky jacket, I hid the golden piece inside an enormous pocket on my right hip, and tried to prop the music box onto the top of the book stand. That proved difficult, as my right side was now several kilos heavier.

Panicking, I did an extreme yoga stretch and managed to return the music box to its original position, before running off towards the front door. Or rather, stumbling up to the door, as my body was now veering to the right under the weight of my pocket.

I continued my impersonation of Quasimodo until I reached my car, where I lay the statue on the back seat. Straightening my spine, I scanned the neighbourhood. No one in sight, and I made a fast exit by jumping behind the wheel and tearing through the streets, stopping at the last mini market to stock up on crisps before hitting the highway.

∽

"Get up!" Matt shouted. "I don't know how I let you talk me into this! You don't even have a shovel!"

I was lying flat on the ground, weary from swirling dirt around.

Dogs can dig a fair-sized hole in no time. My efforts resulted in transforming my hands into a model for Dracula's nail spa, and creating a ditch the size of a teacup.

"I need to hide this, and the best place is under the ground," I lamented. "My aunt's been silent, but she's bound to discover it's gone. She'll eventually phone me; she might even appear on my doorstep."

"I don't want to be around when she gets here." Matt was uneasy. "You stole something from her house, even if it is yours."

As far as my aunt was concerned, I'd learned to expect the unexpected.

As a teenager, I had smoked my first cigarette in her home. A packet of cigarettes had been left in her kitchen. I was alone and lit one, but suddenly heard voices and threw the cigarette out of the window. It set fire to a small, dry shrub, and the person who got a whiff of the smoke, accused me, and subsequently exposed me, was my aunt.

"She could have burned my house down!" she submitted. "Her next step on the ladder of shame will be drugs!" she deduced. "And who knows what after that? She might even end up in prison!"

And that was her final verdict.

A thought occurred to me. Could I end up in prison? For taking what's rightfully mine?

I buried that thought. If only I could bury the statue.

∼

Alone, I sat opposite the likeness of St George, wishing it could talk. We had brought it into my living room and propped it against the dining table, a solid piece of furniture that was guaranteed not to shift position under the statue's weight. Matt had gone home to rest, re-adjust his jeans and probably weigh himself, after his garden workout.

My phone rang. I jumped at the sound, afraid that it was my aunt. It was Matt. We'd met years ago and clicked from the beginning, but had stayed in the friendship zone.

"Hey, how are you doing?" he asked.

"Have a lot of questions in my head. What are you up to?"

"I'm ok, my jeans are a little loose. I lost half a kilo," he replied.

"Some people have all the luck," I murmured.

"What?" he asked.

"Nothing."

Matt was curious. "Say, did your father buy that statue? Or was it a gift? Sorry, just wondering."

"My father told me it was a gift; I think my grandparents gave it to him," I replied.

There was a long pause. "Wait, what do you mean, 'think'? You're not sure who gave it to him?"

"Sure I am." I had a niggling feeling in the depths of my mind, as if a fly had become trapped among my brain cells and was trying to escape.

"Listen, this isn't very clear. Can you remember exactly what you heard?"

As a generalist, I could never retain complete sentences, just the synopsis of a conversation. Is detail that important anyway?

"Hello?"

"I'm still here," I said. "Hey, I'm not a hundred per cent sure of what was said exactly," I confessed.

There was a heavy silence.

"Geez! You went through all that, and got me to dig a crater in your backyard, and you're not sure how your dad got it?"

Matt had a quick temper. His face would turn red, and the combination of red hair and red face made it difficult to see his hairline. I conjured up a mental image of him, but his facial features were a blur against a background of red.

"Don't be upset, I'll remember what happened." We ended the conversation, as my comment had fallen on deaf ears: his and mine.

I stood up and stretched, then sat at my desk to check my emails. There was one I didn't recognise; it was from my aunt. She apologised for not ringing me, as she had the flu, but wanted to chat with me when she was better.

Not sure what to make of this, I hit 'reply' and simply said, "Sure. Hope you feel better soon." Nervous, I waited to learn what she had in store for me.

"This is it," I said to myself. "She'll probably tell me she's going to sue me for stealing her personal property." My nerves were on edge, and I'd started chewing my nails; by the end of the week, they were dangerously close to disappearing.

"Hello?"

It was Clelia. She was over her flu and ready for a chat.

"Hi, um, hi Aunt Clelia. How are you feeling?" My hand was shaking as it clutched the phone.

"Oh, you know, these things come and go. I'm made of iron."

Undeniably.

"My dear, you disappeared the other day and I didn't have a chance to chat with you. It's been so long, and I feel we should speak more often."

"Um, what?"

"Dear, you're not the brightest light bulb," she added. "It would be good to talk about family. We need to chat about your father."

Unsurprisingly.

" Uh huh?"

"Let me explain. Your father was a lovely man," she continued. "He cared for his family, aside from when he was philand.. um."

"What was that?" I asked.

"Good man, a good man," she replied. "And hardworking too."

The back of my head was itching, and my intuition was on red alert.

"But there is a fact about his work that you don't know," she whispered.

Clelia whispering was unusual.

She went on. "During your father's career as a tax specialist, he often took on cases in his own time, in his private practice. You knew that."

My dad often worked as a consultant, that was well known.

"Well, some time ago, one of his clients hired your father. He then made him a.…. a proposition."

"Huh?"

"Rather than reimburse him for services rendered, he offered him a…a gift. Which your father… your father accepted."

Clelia stuttering was unprecedented.

The back of my head was burning. "That gift was the statue you were asking about," she said.

Without a trace of a stutter, her words were now distinct..

"Wait, you mean it wasn't handed down by my grandparents?" I asked.

"Your grandparents? Why would you think that?" she asked. "You really must learn to pay attention when people talk. I feel that conversation spirals in your mind and exits through your ears."

Ignoring my aunt's observations, I tried to connect the dots, suspecting she was going to reveal more.

"The reason we don't talk about it is… the man who gave that item to your father came into possession of it by… theft. It was stolen property. That's why we never talk about it."

She prattled on. This time my aunt's words did spiral in my mind, and evaporated altogether.

~

"What did you say after that?" asked Matt.

"Not much," I replied, mulling over this infinite puzzle.

In a few brief sentences, my aunt had altered the few facts I had of the statue. How did I have the idea that St George was handed down by my grandparents? And why would my dad accept stolen property as a gift? Finally, why had Clelia been keeping it?

"So?" asked Matt. "What are you going to do? You've still got stolen property in your house, except it's stolen from someone you don't even know. That's funny, isn't it?"

"Funny? This isn't funny!" I shouted.

"Relax. Has she realised you snatched it?" he asked.

"I don't think so," I replied. "She would have mentioned it if she had any idea. She also didn't tell me it had been in her home all this time."

"Hmm, that's a lot to take in. Go to sleep; you'll have a clear head in the morning."

~

I hardly slept that night.

I dreamt I was walking through a meadow and sensed I was being followed. Glancing behind, I saw a miniature version of my cousin Jake, whining yet again.

His words were indistinct, and leaning over him, I heard him shriek, "You stole my new phone! Give it back, you bitch!"

Shocked, I turned and ran, while leaning over my right hip, as several kilos of salt crisps had accumulated there.

A log cabin emerged, and on entering it, I found my Aunt Clelia in a rustic kitchen baking a lemon cake. She looked up at me and said, "Where's the light bulb? I need brighter light in here. You're not the smartest electrician I've come across!"

Electrician?

I left the cabin and ran into the meadow, where I saw my father. He spoke to me, but I could only hear the sound of a siren. "I have to go!" I shouted. "The police are going to find me!" The shrill sound of the siren was piercing my eardrums. I woke up to the sound of my ringing phone.

"Hello? Is that you, Matt?"

"Hey, how did you sleep?"

"Oh, terrible, terrible dream!." I replied. "And I saw my father in the dream. He was talking to me, but I couldn't hear a word."

"Listen, you've got a lot of your dad's personal stuff, don't you? Old letters, emails?" asked Matt. "Maybe we'll solve a few mysteries. I'll drop by in a couple of hours."

There was no other way of tracking down answers; my mum had passed away a couple of years before my dad, and I didn't believe I'd glean any more information from Clelia.

"Yes, please come over," I said.

"Your dad kept a hell of a lot of paperwork," said Matt. We were sifting through the contents of several brown envelopes.

"Yeah, my dad couldn't get used to the internet. He used it at the office, but outside work preferred the old-fashioned way of pen on paper."

Letters, memos, journals, many of which had yellowed over time. I discovered a father's day card I'd sent him many years ago, with my scribbles and happy emojis, and old shopping lists he'd stashed into an envelope.

"What's this?" asked Matt.

It was a printed email sent to my dad. The sender was Paul Markland, a name that sounded vaguely familiar.

"What does it say?"

"This is interesting," I replied. "He's talking about a statue in the email."

Matt had also uncovered a handwritten letter by my father addressed to Paul Markland.

I read through it. "I remember where I've heard his name

before. He and my aunt had a relationship some years ago. She's been a widow for a long time, and met this guy maybe six years ago. Apparently my dad did work for him."

At the bottom of a stack of correspondence, there was a letter addressed to my father with a more recent date; this one was from Aunt Clelia. In it, she claimed that her now ex-partner, Paul Markland, had removed from her premises a valuable item she had purchased, a solid gold, gem-laden statue of St George. She believed he did that to pay for business services my father had rendered him, as Paul's finances were dwindling. In the letter, she was requesting that the statue kindly be returned to her.

I showed the letter to Matt.

"You know what this means, don't you?" he asked. "Your aunt is the person the statue was 'stolen' from. You've done full circle. St George belongs to your aunt."

I stared into space. It was starting to make sense. My dad had become ill shortly after he was gifted the statue, and was mostly in hospital. Clelia wanted her golden treasure returned but had no way of collecting it.

"Your dad probably wanted to return it but didn't get a chance," Matt continued. "And as for your grandparents being involved, I think you imagined that."

I barely blinked. "Matt, I need a favour. You have to help me take this back to Clelia's house."

His deadpan expression made me edgy.

"Did you hear me?"

He glared at me, and said, "What kind of help do you mean?", punching his words into the air.

"Oh, don't be upset!" I said. His face was turning red, a shade dangerously close to the colour of his hair.

"What exactly are you suggesting?" he demanded.

"Let me work on it."

"Of all your screwy schemes, this has to be borderline psycho!"

We were driving to Clelia's house, and Matt was still pissed off.

Set in his ways, he had a temper that would flare up over trivial things. Having said that, this scenario was anything but trivial, and I appreciated that he was there.

"Keep her occupied, I won't be long," I said, feigning confidence. Anxious, I hid my uneven nails, and talked about TV comedies to lighten the mood.

We parked in Clelia's driveway. She spied us through her bay window, and rushed out into the garden. "My dears, welcome!"

Examining Matt from top to toe with a rare twinkle in her eye, she exclaimed, "What surprising news!" And turning to me said, "Aren't you the mysterious lady!"

"Yes, Aunt Clelia. After I called you to announce our wonderful news, we wanted to pay you a visit; that's why I suggested coming out here today. And so… this is Matt. My fiancé."

Matt looked uncomfortable, his brow deepening. "Hi… um, hello," he stammered. "Lovely to meet you, and thank you, ah, thanks for inviting us here today."

"Oh, my pleasure, to be sure. Such a joyful event! Come in, do come in."

We strolled towards the front door, Matt with his arm around my waist, and a briefcase in my hand between us.

"My, my, you are the lovebirds," Clelia commented with a wry smile.

My briefcase weighed several kilos, and I leaned on Matt for support.

As we settled into the living room, Clelia's eye fell onto my briefcase beside my feet.

"My, my, you are the studious one, aren't you," she commented. "Did you bring your work with you?"

"Oh, it's just my laptop. I need to go over a few figures tonight," I replied, averting my gaze to admire her Persian rug.

"Of course, of course. I'll bring out some nibbles and pumpkin pie," Clelia gushed. "What will you drink?"

"Oh, water for me," I said.

"Stiff whiskey," whispered Matt.

"What was that, dear?" she asked him.

"Spritz, thanks."

She stood up to fetch the drinks, when I said, "Aunt Clelia, I'm going to pop into the bathroom for a sec?"

"Of course, my dear."

I stood up, and Matt stood up with me. Clelia looked at us, raising an eyebrow. "Are you both going to the bathroom?"

"Oh, no," I giggled, making a nervous, childish sound. "He loves being close to me. Just won't let go!"

With an eyebrow still raised, she stared at my briefcase, as Matt had picked it up.

"And will your briefcase also accompany you on your way to the bathroom?" she asked.

"Oh, he-he… Well, I usually pop my makeup into it. Where else can a working girl keep it?" surprising myself with my quick response.

"Very well then, I'll prepare a few things in the kitchen," she replied, although judging by her pursed lips, she didn't seem impressed.

Matt cast me a sideways glance, and mouthed, "Are you okay?" I nodded, as we proceeded towards the bathroom with my briefcase. Leaving Matt behind, I entered Clelia's bedroom. So far, so good.

The music box was not on the book stand. In a frenzy, I snooped around the entire room, pinpointing any flat surface, while listening to the faint conversation from the living room.

"Well, my dear, you are quite the catch," Clelia complimented Matt.

What was she saying? Did she comment on his watch?

"If only I were 20 years younger," she admitted, with a crafty tone in her voice.

"Uh, yeah, uh…"

Was Matt lost for words? Very unlike him. What were they saying?

Clelia must have taken the key from the music box to open the trunk. She'd know it was gone, and that I was the thief. A hundred scenarios crossed my mind, each with a disastrous conclusion.

I rested my hand on top of the book stand and felt something just out of reach. Swishing it to the front, the music box skidded up to my face, crashing into my nose.

Stifling a yelp, I opened the music box to find the key was still there, and in a flash darted across the room to return St George to the safety of the trunk.

Proud of my skilful precision, I neatly repositioned the music box with its key onto the book stand, knocking aside a pink fluffy bauble in the process. The bauble flew past me, hit the door and disappeared out of the room.

I gasped. My plan was going awry. I poked my head out of the bedroom to see the bauble on the hallway floor.

Clelia's laughter reached my ears, as I crept into the hallway to retrieve the wayward bauble.

"I'll bring some napkins and nuts, Matt," she oozed, rushing into the kitchen.

My plan had deviated totally off course. I flattened myself against the wall next to an antique redwood cupboard, which my aunt had plonked in the hallway many years ago. I'd always hated this massive piece, but was now grateful for its protection. From my hideaway, I caught sight of Clelia's flushed, excited face as she fluttered into the kitchen.

I seized the fluffy bauble, when I heard the front door opening.

"Mum, I'm here," squealed my cousin, Jake.

Hidden behind the cupboard's side panel, I moved slightly so my right eye could monitor the living room scene.

Jake had entered the living room, and on seeing Matt, stood motionless near the couch.

"Hi," said Matt.

"Who are you?" asked Jake, shyly.

"I'm Matt. I'm your cousin's fiancé."

"Which cousin? asked Jake, lifting his head upwards. "Matt? I've heard that name before… Ugh! Salt City got engaged?" Jake spat out, staring straight ahead and frowning in denial.

Salt City? Wtf? Well, I suppose I do relish my savouries.

"I mean, yeah, nice," said Jake, attempting a grin. "You're cute," he added, unsure of himself, shifting his gaze to Matt's shoes.

Cute? Flushed faces? What is going on in the living room?

"Uh, um, I think your mum's bringing the nuts," said Matt.

Are they still talking about nuts?

Clelia entered the living room, and on seeing her son, stiffened slightly and pursed her lips. "Jake, go and make some calls with your new phone. Stop bothering the man."

Unhappy with his mother's instructions, Jake meandered down the hallway, dragging his feet, and examining his socks on the way.

My throat was parched. I slid along the wall, hoping I could hide in one of the spare rooms before Jake finished inspecting his footwear.

He suddenly looked up and saw me, jumping like a startled deer. "What are you doing here?" he asked, screwing up his nose.

"Me? Oh, uh, I was in the… the bathroom."

"Weren't you standing next to that cupboard?"

"Cupboard? No, the bathroom, bathroom. I've got no business with your mum's bedroom. I mean cupboard!" I mumbled, my mouth dry.

He shrugged and went into his bedroom.

My aunt never considered me a bright spark, but truth was, her son had blown a fuse long ago.

With the bauble back in place, I grabbed my briefcase and jetted into the living room.

There, I witnessed a scene unlike any other. Sitting next to each other, my aunt was leaning towards Matt, while he was leaning away. They vaguely resembled the Leaning Tower of Pisa. Their expressions were in opposition; my aunt had one of glee, while Matt had one of fear.

"Aunt Clelia!" I commanded, a trickle of Matt's temper running through my veins.

Surprised, she straightened herself, smoothed her blouse and surveyed the snacks.

"Dear, will you have some nuts?" she asked.

"Dearest," I replied, "it's time for us to go."

"What? You only arrived a moment ago! And what took you so long in the bathroom?" she complained, clearly annoyed that Matt would be leaving so soon.

"My dear aunt, it's my work. Unexpected phone call, what to do?" I replied.

My improv was on fire, and judging from Matt's smile, I had his stamp of approval.

"If you must," she replied, sheepishly.

Matt put his arm around me, and we walked to the front door.

"Goodbye, Aunt Clelia. It was good to see you."

We left her standing by the front door, and as we got into the car, Matt said, "Go for an audition. That was a five-star performance!" He laughed.

"Truth is, I amazed myself."

"St George okay?" he asked.

"He's in the trunk, and better off there."

"Feel better now?" he added. "You're gonna forget about who owns what, and where everything belongs?"

I looked ahead without speaking; he glanced at me and rolled his eyes.

"By the way, what happened to your nose?" he asked.

"Forget it."

THE END

Enchantment

Adelaide Hunter

Madame Ophidian adjusted her red headscarf, sat down across from me at the small table, and focused pale ancient eyes on mine. She had a gentle face that wore wrinkles like gullies. My heart went out to her, dressed in shabby, thin clothing, with remnants of vivid colour peeping around fringed edges. She didn't say much, just waited for time to settle and the vagaries of thought to disperse. On the table between us rested some cards, a silver chain with a deep red stone and Madame's gnarled hands. The flame from a single candle flickered in the darkened tent, set slightly apart from others at the county fair. Madame began whispering a chant while I fidgeted in my chair a little, trying to reign in scattered thoughts and reflected on how life led me here.

My family used to sing together - especially in the car when we went on road trips. Our singing was quite a contrast to the sombre dirge Madame was mumbling to me now. Once, our family was taking a trip up North to Byron Bay during the school holidays. Ryan was driving, I was navigating, and Quinn was playing a version of Trivial Pursuit with celebrity trivia thrown in as a bonus. The celebrity trivia usually ended up being linked to some version of the latest popular songs that only a fourteen-year-old could know. Quinn had it all covered while Ryan and I scratched our heads, trying to guess the names of the bands that sang those songs and name the songs too. We knew the songs by heart - Quinn played them in his room and even a shut door didn't tone down the volume much. But when Quinn challenged us to sing these songs, we always laughed, knowing it was outside the comfort zone of our age bracket. Instead, we fell back onto good old favourites that Ryan and I sang to Quinn when he was a little boy. He always gave into this with as much grace as a suffering teenager could muster.

"Ok Mum, let's try those old songs from back in the day that you and Dad know," Quinn said, grinning.

I turned to face him in the back seat of the car and raised my eyebrows.

"We know you secretly love singing these Quinn, and now's the chance while your mates aren't around to hear you," I teased.

"You are my Sunshine," he began sotto voce, throwing out the challenge with crinkly eyes.

It was our special crazy family time and two-part harmony featured in those songs where we were able to make it work. I took over the melody while Ryan and Quinn harmonised softly to accompany me. After each song, we always ended up laughing together.

"Seriously guys, I think we've found a niche brand that we could market. After all, how many parents sing harmony with their teenage sons these days? I think the girls would love it!"

"Better not give up our day jobs son," Ryan would respond and the banter would go back and forth.

It was corny and sweet - my man and my son becoming a man. Life was good.

And now my nerves were shattered. It was like living in a void, as though a door to a dark world had been opened - one that I had never known and could not have imagined to its full extent. The ache inside was unbearable. If only I were twenty years down the track away from this moment, maybe life would be better. But now I could not even imagine a better life, let alone keep up a facade of pretending to live one. My old friend Samantha was the only person who seemed to understand.

Samantha insisted I seek help from Madame in order to help piece me back together. The car accident happened just over a year ago now. I was left with serious physical injuries that would, with time, heal. I also had been rendered mute since the accident and the psychiatrist said that this too would eventually come good. Thrice weekly sessions with a speech therapist who specialised in post-traumatic cases like mine, yielded nothing - not even a whisper. I spent hours doing voice homework in front of the computer - practicing exercises designed to coax sound from my larynx. Sometimes I felt like my voice had to jump over a canyon so wide that it was impossible. The closest I came to producing a sound was with Frank - a professional singer who also mentored students through examinations at the Sydney Conservatorium of Music. Frank understood the connection between music and the soul more than any of the therapists. Perhaps this was the key. My hibernating voice was grateful too and for the first time after almost making a sound, I felt the tingle of real hope that one day I would be able to sing again.

∽

Still, after the year had passed, despite many hours of therapy and the promise of sound, my voice remained silent. A wise psychiatrist suggested that in cases like mine, the sole survivor often left something of themselves at the scene of the trauma, keeping a living connection to the dead. In the land of the living before the accident, my voice united with the voices of my family, especially when we sang together. Maybe this was more important than I ever realised. Had I left my voice with Ryan and Quinn?

Their tragic deaths left me crumbling and perhaps that's why the psychiatrist's words resonated with me. My longing for them both was a powerful hurt - it was as much physical as emotional, and in a way, spiritual too. Ryan and Quinn were embedded within every single cell of my body, and their deaths ripped the membrane of life from me so violently in that horrific instant. It left me as an empty shell. Their voices and mine would never join in harmony again. I missed them with an unbearable sorrow. Bitter tears would not bring them back, no matter how much I wished and prayed. Deep down, I knew this to be true.

In the shadow of grief, I sensed that my voice was waiting for the right time to come back, and would not present itself until then. My caring but bossy friend Samantha, however, held the directly opposing view, and thought that by now, I should be speaking normally. After all, a whole year had passed. For me, it wasn't the time so much as the loss of being able to sing. If I could only sing again, music would connect me once more to my men, and the crooked seam of sorrow might begin to mend.

Samantha visited Madame for nine months, during which there were several readings of palms and an exchange of hard earned cash. Her fortune really had changed. Her failing business turned the corner and took off. She was earning big dollars and moving in circles of the rich and famous. Even Samantha herself had changed. What was it about her that left me with a lingering sense of unease? Something nebulous, but perhaps it was my imagination mixed with a little envy. I remained skeptical about taking Samantha's advice, yet her life was the life of a winner and mine, simply one who exists. The evidence stood before me and I couldn't refute it. As time passed, weariness wore away at me and my reserve diminished. I began to ruminate that if Madame had helped Samantha, she might be able to help me too. Maybe I could dig myself out of that black hole that fate had dug. Madame continued murmuring her doleful tune when an old caution surfaced.

It was a niggling thought - a vague memory of my mother's warning not to meddle in such things. She said something about opening a door, but never explained any further. Remembering this, my fingers reached to touch the familiar engraved pattern of her rose gold locket resting on my chest, as was my habit. Madame's eyes glanced fleetingly at my locket, and her left eyebrow twitched almost imperceptibly. The locket was a soothing balm as I worked it between my index finger and thumb. The smooth surface punctuated by the ridge of the engraved heart connected me to my mother, who died ten years ago.

The locket was handed down through the generations, from mother to daughter. It was gifted to me by my mother when I turned twenty-one and I would gift it to my daughter on her twenty-first birthday. But I didn't have a daughter... and my family was dead. I sighed a weary sigh and longed to be some version of normal again. Although Frank had almost managed to draw a sound from me, I was tired and weary. Perhaps it was a soul problem, and I needed a soul doctor. Besides, how much more therapy could I take? Casting aside my hesitation, I ended up sitting opposite Madame in the little tent at the edge of the fair.

Madame Ophidian continued mumbling her mournful chant in the little tent, with the flicker of candlelight licking the walls. Her voice travelled across a chasm to reach me. She seemed to understand me even though my words were lost. I sat there and listened like an obedient child, hands resting in my lap and thoughts becalmed. Her words sang a gentle song, weaving a spell, drawing me in. Words that were hushed at first became deeper and more sonorous. I floated on those words and followed them round and around,

> *Slipping and Swirling,*
> *Curling and Whirling,*
> *Dreaming and Drowning,*
> *Enchanted.*

Words sailed along the coast of my inner being, pushing and probing, gently at first and then more insistent. The safe harbour of my very self was being tested, and I felt pinpricks of cold sweat creep up the back of my neck. Some kind of question was being asked, but I didn't understand. I was becoming entangled in a web of sticky words and when I tried to resist, an unspoken threat compelled me to consider something not yet clear. I was drawn into that fog of words, little by little. Enthralled.

Madame Ophidian's eyes narrowed and the air in the room shifted. It was heavier. She brought her face closer to mine, and I smelled the fetid stench of decay. I recoiled slightly. Her words grew more forceful with a hint of menace. She was toying with me… waiting. I tried to move, but my limbs were like stone. Ensnared.

Her words gathered force now and a barrage of them beat down upon me. I stood my ground, shaking in this war of wills, and managed to hold the viper at bay. Madame drew her trump card, twirling the deep red stone in front of my eyes that were becoming mesmerised by the mirrored candlelight glinting in each facet. My stomach churned with a fear most primal and drawing a mighty effort, I closed my eyes. A burning pain immediately stung my eyelids and a lick of sweat bathed my forehead. The storm of words swelled to a tempest. My will resisted, but despair began to gnaw at its edges.

The pain in my eyelids stung wildly now - like a thousand bees' searing signature. I knew that if I opened my eyes, the pain would cease, but I would then be completely vulnerable to the mercy of Madame Ophidian. And she had no mercy.

Madame Ophidian went for the jugular. A wordless choice was presented to me and I shivered. I now understood. It was a contract of blood, promising health, wealth and honour - all for one simple exchange. The pressure to consent was unbearable and my will was crumbling. I could hardly breathe. How easy it would be to just open my eyes and submit. I wanted a normal life back, and I wanted it desperately. Could I agree to this exchange for now but retrieve my soul later? No longer could I bear this agony - it was time to surrender.

As I stood on the precipice of darkness about to make my choice, the sound of a bell jingled through the tent. It came from a small child riding by on a push-bike. She sang an old nursery rhyme - one that Mother sang to me as a child. The pain in my eyelids eased, and I gingerly opened my eyes. Single musical notes - golden and shining, floated into the tent and circled around the small table between Madame and me. The air shifted again and was lighter this time. I breathed in deeply. The golden notes doubled and harmony filled the tent. Beautiful music, together with the sheer joy of that memory, mingled together. It was enough to interrupt the enchantment, for the time of a breath. My right hand tingled, and I began dragging the leaden limb to my chest where the locket lay.

Madame sensed the disruption in the atmosphere and swirled the red stone frantically, leaning in closer, muttering strange words under her foul, stinking breath. Her eyes, now black as onyx, intensified their gaze upon me as she summoned help from the powerful unseen. A charcoal mist filled the tent and battled with the golden harmonies, a strange and macabre dance. The darkening mist swelled to a squall, whirling about the tent with fury. It swallowed the golden notes one by one. I struggled to see through the blackness, all the time my fingers inching towards my chest. Madame was gaining the upper hand, and I knew with every fibre of my being that I must choose now.

At last, my fingers reached the rose gold locket and held fast onto it. Time stretched and rang through the ages, calling those from my past, some whom I knew and others who were before me but whose blood lived in me now. I held my breath, suspended on the brink of a curious dimension. Generations of aunts, cousins, sisters, grandmothers and mothers surrounded me and breathed a gentle perfume through the tent. Flames from the candle danced a desperate dance as Madame Ophidian's eyes glittered.

I looked into those two pools of the abyss and made my choice.

Madame's once peaceful face showed its utter displeasure. She was ugly and ferocious, a tower of malice, intent on harm now that she had lost control. She leaned over the table towards me and reached to grab my locket. I shrank back into the chair as her fingers swooped past my chest, clutching nothing but air. My nostrils flared and a spark lit a fire within. She will not have my locket. She will not have my soul. Fighting against weak knees and a shaking body, I gripped the table and stood tall and straight. We faced each other, will against will. Realising that within my blood lived a powerful force - generations of women wise and strong, I summoned my dormant voice and cried "BEGONE!"

The candle flames withered and died, leaving wisps of smoke to drown in the perfume of roses that filled the space. The black mist cleared and the golden notes returned to shimmer in the air. The enchantment was shattered!

Madame Ophidian slumped into her chair, weary and deflated like a dried up prune. I heard beautiful music from the golden notes surrounding me. The music seeped into my bones and made its way into my heart. I looked at Madame with pity, knowing that she did not know how to love. Turning my back to her, I waved to the fading generations of women as they made their way to the other place. And as I looked closer, I saw the arms of those women around two glorious men, a father and son, who turned to me and smiled.

THE END

Irina Gladushchenko lives in the Sydney Eastern suburbs. Her passions are family and wellbeing. She believes in human's ability to heal and to achieve harmonious living. Irina's short stories focus on various aspects of the human condition and reflect on lived experiences. This is her fourth anthology.

The Invisible Cloud

Irina Gladushchenko

Professor Liraz Pegany finally finished her last class of the term and eagerly began to get ready for her overseas trip. A frequent traveller, there was nothing she had forgotten – clothes packed, travel documents prepared, weather checked. All was ready for her departure in precisely 16 hours and 16 minutes.

She found herself in an unfamiliar 'nothing more to do' state with a few hours to go before she needed to go to bed. She considered catching up with a friend but was worried this would overstimulate her and take her past her intended bedtime.

Reading was out of the question as her eyes were feeling tired after the intensity of the last six months. What a ride it had been! Liraz made a mental note to reduce the number of research students she would supervise in the future.

I could really use a pick-me-up right now, Liraz thought.

She decided to plug into holiday mode immediately: she took three full breaths, turned on Spotify and started to move and sway to her favourite playlist. Her movements made her aware of how tired she was and how much restoring needed to be done but, as one of her clients would describe, it also brought in so much oomph.

And there it was! Recognisable from the first millisecond, a short tender intro followed by the 'Khaaaaa' sound of "How Deep Is Your Love" by The Bee Gees.

Her memories from their concert in 2000 came flooding back with the harmonious melody — the gentle midwinter sunset with perfectly shaped clouds coloured in pale purple, Adriatic blue and intense pink, and a sense of being one with her husband Zak in a stadium full of strangers. Liraz felt grateful for the kind of connection they had with each other that was so sublime and almost ethereal; like they were part of an invisible cloud. Oh, how many "I love yous" they exchanged that night and how easy it was for her back then to express her feelings! She wished it could still be that way but it felt like she had lost her ability to communicate with him the way she used to.

Reconnecting with her lightness through her memories felt inspiring, and it made her want to reward her body, so an Epsom salt bath was next on the evening's program. Candles, raindrop sounds and a warm, whole-body embrace by the water made her feel even more at peace. She felt comfortable and safe – this is what an unborn baby must feel like inside the womb, she reflected.

Waking up to bird song a little before the alarm the next morning, Liraz felt profoundly rested. The smell of fresh air and the tender playfulness of the sun's first rays made her feel young and cheerful. She smiled at the new day, and the new day smiled back at her. This time tomorrow, she would be on the other side of the world. Again, she could feel the tingling of excitement anticipating her reunion with Zak.

It had felt strange not to talk to him before her departure. As a photographer and lecturer, he often travelled to the world's most remote corners to capture the perfect shots. They had been married for 27 years, and this was the first time they were not leaving on holiday together, as Liraz's schedule clashed with his photography trip along the Silk Road in Tajikistan. Liraz especially regretted missing this expedition — it sounded like the opportunity of a lifetime — as she always accompanied Zak in the past.

He had no phone or internet connection most of the time, and he couldn't even share a single photo before customs cleared it. Not being able to exchange in their usual way was challenging for such visual communicators, so the three conversations they managed to have over the last two months felt somewhat fragmented and unengaging. But most importantly, besides of the obstacles of technology and distance, their cloud connection was not there.

Liraz checked her emails while waiting to board her flight when she saw one from an unknown sender in her junk folder. She was about to delete it when she noticed the name "Marianne" in the subject line. Her heart sank, and an electrical charge went down her spine. She knew to prepare for some sad news. Marianne was someone of significance in her life. Their connection began many years earlier during Liraz's placement before graduating as a counsellor, but they hadn't communicated much in recent times.

Liraz paused for a moment to find the depth of her breath, and then started to read. It was from Marianne's daughter, Michaela, advising that her mum had passed away. It read:

After a debilitating time with an autoimmune disease, she eventually slipped away peacefully at the local hospital. I was by her side with Dad, my husband, and our two kids. She had said many times recently that she was ready to go and made that decision with her eyes open and heart at peace. She is now enjoying a well-earned rest.

Marianne was Liraz's very first counselling client outside the classroom. As if it were yesterday, she recalled how nervous she felt before that very first session and how that feeling shifted once Marianne arrived and they looked into each other's eyes. A few years after she graduated, Liraz continued to support Marianne through her own counselling studies. Their boundaries transformed with time, and they established a unique, obligation-free bond.

They shared a cloud of serendipitous moments, where they learnt the art of trust and consciously cultivated a child-like curiosity. They would send each other photos of the full moon at precisely the same moment, they enrolled in the same short courses, bumped into each other at events, or just called each other at exactly the right time. Liraz and Marianne had their last get together three months earlier when they talked about every aspect of the end of one's life journey, soaking in each emotion as it arose. They cried openly. And they also laughed hard. They reflected on their first sessions when Marianne complained about the lack of affection and emotional availability her husband offered her at that time, and how he became her primary carer and was now the epitome of love itself at this stage of her journey. "The power of intention!" they exclaimed in unison, visiting their serendipity cloud once again.

Even in her debilitated state, Marianne maintained her calmness and empathic ways, and her emotional intelligence reached a whole new level. She suddenly had the need and energy to share.

"You know, one day he was helping me to get dressed in our bedroom, and I looked away, embarrassed and angry at my helplessness. But then I saw him in our built-in mirrors, how lovingly he was tending to my body, even though I could feel nothing at all. It was such a profound experience, and something clicked in me — I felt love for myself, for him, and for our special connection. Life plays this game of disconnecting and reconnecting with us, doesn't it? How is it for you and Zak these days?"

"Work in progress," Liraz sighed.

As she allowed herself to start grieving for her beautiful friend Marianne, her quest became very clear. She didn't want to wait for a life crisis to be able to love again. In that state of rawness, she promised herself to act now.

Liraz was finally on her way to Germany to meet Zak, and from there they would travel to Holland together to visit their son Jack and meet his fiancée, Zoe. During the first leg, she had a whole row of empty seats to herself and was relieved to have time to reflect and relax. She checked that her journal and pen were in her seat pocket and stared out the window, admiring the art of the clouds. The warmth and brightness of the reflective light was extraordinary — it lured Liraz into the realm of nothingness even more profoundly, where 'beyond clouds' became 'beyond thoughts' for her.

She woke up trying to remember her dream, but it evaporated with all the excitement of the breakfast service as the plane approached her first stop in Hong Kong. The only aspect she retained was the feeling of softness.

After stretching her legs and enjoying the most delicious fresh tropical fruit juice at the airport, Liraz joined the other passengers on board for the final leg of her journey. This plane was totally packed — no more spacious luxury! On her left was a beautiful older lady and on her right was a very serious-looking young man.

The conversation with the lady started to flow straight after their introductions. Her name was Anne-Marie, the reverse of her friend Marianne's name! *Serendipity is still here, now beyond the human form*, Liraz smiled to herself, feeling reassured.

They landed at Frankfurt Airport but after nearly two hours on the tarmac had still not been allowed to disembark. Oxygen levels were low, and the collective energy felt tense. There had been no explanation, no information, and no movement onboard permitted. Anne-Marie's mobile rang — it was her daughter who was meant to meet her in Budapest. She quickly informed Anne-Marie that there had been a shooting at Frankfurt Airport while their plane was landing. As a result, airport operations were paralysed, passengers in the airport were evacuated, and high-security investigations were underway.

A short while later, they were allowed to disembark and move to the secure transit area. Somehow, Liraz got separated from Anne-Marie but then saw her sitting in a corner next to a young gentleman bandaging her thumb.

"What happened?" Liraz asked.

"My dear, old age has happened to me! I tripped on the escalator and cut my thumb. But please, meet my rescuer, Pete. Not only did he carry all our belongings, but he also saved me from embarrassment.

Liraz, are you okay, my friend?"

"Yes," Liraz nodded, slowly returning to her senses...

Anne-Marie was now a chatterbox, sharing every detail of her fall and how all these beautiful people helped find antiseptic and fabric pieces to stop her bleeding. She then recalled how this brought about her childhood memories of bombings during the siege of Budapest. One of their fellow passengers brought them sandwiches and hot tea. Even in such a bizarre setting, Anne-Marie's company offered Liraz a sense of comfort. *It feels like we've known each other forever,* thought Liraz, *or maybe it is the way my grief for Marianne is showing up.*

Liraz was observing their situation as though they were in a slow-motion movie when suddenly, she was brought straight back to her body by an incoming call — it was her son Jack telling her that all was under control. Zak's flight had been redirected to Düsseldorf. Frankfurt was still closed, but arrangements had been made to transport everyone from Liraz's group once security gave the all-clear to leave the airport. She felt alive again. She thanked Jack with a broad smile on her face as she thought, *my little one is now the leader of our clan.*

She exchanged details with Anne-Marie and a few other fellow travellers, thanking each of them for their presence and support.

As the bus approached Düsseldorf station, she was becoming more and more impatient. The need to see Zak had become an obsessive thought. *Twenty years of therapy working on codependency — down the drain!* she thought. The bus stopped; she looked around, and the very first thing she noticed was a massive cloud of balloons in her favourite colours and familiar old runners underneath it. She laughed at the spectacle.

They programmed the GPS with their son's address, but they were so distracted sharing stories and exchanging passionate glances that they kept missing their turns. They were driving through the countryside, and Liraz was mesmerised by the natural beauty surrounding them. Suddenly she saw something intriguing out of the corner of her eye. She started to turn around to have a better look when Zak suddenly pressed hard on the brakes.

"What's the matter?" asked Liraz.

"The road looks like it narrows down a lot."

Liraz checked the GPS. "It shows a wide road ahead – maybe the GPS just wanted us to drive through here?"

Zak started to drive again, but nearly ran into a huge pine tree in front of an entry into a dark forest. He miraculously managed to turn off into a clearing at the last moment. He started to manoeuvre through a seven-point turn while Liraz kept staring hard at something in front of them.

Suddenly, she could no longer contain herself and screamed, "Stop the car!"

"What? What is the matter? Did we run something over?"

"No," she replied, rushing out. "This is just unbelievable!"

She started to run towards the field. Zak parked the car and walked towards the field where she had run. As he approached, he saw a fluffy cloud rolling over the field but there was no sign of Liraz. Then, just as he started to worry, the sun came out, and the cloud burst right before his eyes and Liraz suddenly appeared under a rainbow.

"Here she is, my crazy woman!" he said tenderly, hugging her around the shoulders.

They were now standing together under the delicate rainbow arch, tears running down their cheeks as they quietly reflected on this eventful day, each counting their blessings.

After a while, she turned to face him and whispered, looking into his eyes, "I love you more than life, Zak!"

THE END

Marjorie Banks has been writing short stories and poetry for several decades. Marjorie has enjoyed writing since her school days. Before Weaving Words, Marjorie's work was selected to featured in Anthology: Short Stories Vol 1 by the Sydney School of Arts & Humanities. When not at her typewriter, Marjorie enjoys gardening, bushwalking and puzzles.

June's Casseroles

Marjorie Banks

June made casseroles. That was what she did. For the bereaved, for new parents, for people who had just moved house, for friends and neighbours recuperating from various conditions. June couldn't recall when it had first started, but it just seemed the right thing to do. She'd still send a condolence note or a get-well-soon card. But there's not a lot you can do with a card if you're laid up with a broken leg.

A casserole, though, is a practical thing. It can be eaten. It nourishes. And the people receiving June's casseroles were usually in need of nourishment. Elderly widowers who couldn't cook more than a can of soup and sat about all day, alone with their loss. New mothers, so sleep-deprived they literally forgot to eat. People of all types and ages, home-bound and recuperating, barely able to stand long enough to make a cup of tea.

"I don't know how you do it," June's friend Dolly would say. "I never know how you find the time."

Time wasn't really the problem. Finding casserole dishes was June's biggest challenge. Often they weren't returned or would show up on her doorstep months later, occasionally accompanied by an apologetic note. Sometimes the wrong dish was returned. June felt no qualms about keeping and reusing these. They'd find their way home eventually, like a lost cat. Someone would spot it and claim it, or return it to the right person.

You could, of course, use disposable tin-foil trays. But June wasn't fond of these. They didn't hold up well. They were saggy. Saggy and soggy. Instead when she ran out she scoured the local thrift and charity shops for anything suitable. On more than a few occasions she had recognised one of her own dishes in there.

"Didn't you buy a dish just like that last month?" one of the women who worked in the Red Cross shop asked. "Getting a collection together, are you?"

"Perhaps she's selling them on the internet," her colleague suggested. "My grandson says there are a lot of china collectors on there." She was a large, cosy-looking woman in a fluffy hand-knitted grey cardigan. They were all volunteers, these women. June always wondered how charity shops managed to donate any proceeds to their good causes. They must make barely enough to pay their rent and electricity bills.

"It is similar, isn't it?" June commented, regarding the design of orange and brown flowers. She didn't like to explain that it was the same one. It had contained a beef casserole which she'd dropped around to old Arthur Fellows, after Madge had passed on. His relatives had bundled him off to an old people's home within weeks, packing up and clearing out the house of all his possessions. They lived too far away, they had said, and couldn't care for him. There was no suggestion of moving Arthur nearer to them.

Along with her casserole dish, June had an idea that a set of patterned teacups displayed in the charity shop window had been Madge's. They might not have been Royal Doulton but they'd cost more in their day than the few coins they were now selling for. And Madge had doubtless been proud of them and brought them out for tea parties. Now they were someone else's second-hand junk. How very quickly they had been discarded.

June wasn't the only person who made casseroles, of course. There were many other people in the community who did so. June was simply the most consistent, and her casseroles among the best. Nor did June only cook casseroles. She was a dab hand with cakes and sweet treats, regularly baking for the church cake stall and the parish ladies' group. Everything except rock cakes, because that was Phyllis Davenport's speciality.

June had made the transgression of producing a plate of rock cakes many years ago when she had first moved to the neighbourhood. She was to learn that Phyllis was "known for her rock cakes" and took great affront at anyone else trying to eclipse them. June steered tactfully clear of buns and currants after that. Chocolate cake and jam tarts seemed safe enough. She also made a point of expressing delight over Phyllis's rock cakes - even though they nearly broke a tooth - and asking her for the recipe.

It was a grey and windy Wednesday morning when June dropped off a chicken and mushroom casserole to the new family at number five. She thought chicken might be safe enough. A lot of people didn't eat pork these days, at least many of the new types of people moving into the neighbourhood. She had also heard that even beef might be a problem. So chicken it was.

A young man opened the door to June's knock. He wore glasses and looked to be in his early thirties. "I'm June, from two houses along," she introduced herself. "Just welcoming you to the neighbourhood. And a casserole, in case you haven't got your fridge and cooker sorted out yet."

He looked mildly bewildered. "That's very kind." June handed him the dish and quickly went on her way. She didn't like to impose. People moving in were usually drowning in crates and boxes and even having someone in for a cup of tea could be troublesome. If they were the neighbourly types, they'd probably return the dish with an invitation to tea. If not, no harm done.

Back in her kitchen she put the kettle on then busied herself looking through a new cookbook she had treated herself to. Most of the casseroles June cooked were simple, traditional recipes. Bereaved and convalescent people needed comforting and familiar fare, and fancy food didn't seem quite appropriate. A Beef Stroganoff was about as exotic as it got. But June sometimes had a hankering to try something more ambitious, which she got the chance to when Dolly came for supper.

Dolly had a weakness for French food, particularly dishes rich with cream and butter. But her husband was a retired doctor who kept a rather sharp eye on her waistline. In his defence, Dolly's blood pressure wasn't all that it could be and she did have a tendency to embonpoint. June sympathised. It was hard to find a middle ground between Stanley's tenet of strict moderation in everything with Dolly's philosophy of "a lot of what you fancy does you good".

So Dolly indulged her illicit gastronomic desires at June's house. That evening June was planning a recipe from the new cookbook: Chicken à la Normande. Featuring cream, whisky, bacon and cider, it was certainly not on Stanley's approved list.

There was a knock at the door. June put down the book and went to answer it. The young man from two houses down was on the doorstop, holding the casserole she had given him. He looked embarrassed.

"Hello again," June greeted him.

"Hello. This is very awkward because it was so very kind of you to offer us this. But I'm afraid we're vegetarians. I didn't like to waste it, since it looks very fine, so I thought it best to return it. I do hope you're not offended."

He stood there, still holding the dish and looking so anxious that June smiled to reassure him. "No offence taken. I'm only sorry I didn't know. Why don't you come in?"

"Thank you." He followed her through the hall and into the kitchen, carrying the casserole.

June offered him a cup of tea as the kettle had just boiled. He accepted and she poured out two cups. "Milk?" she asked, with some hesitation.

"Yes. Please. We're only vegetarian, not vegan. In fact…" he looked even more shamefaced "…we're actually not completely vegetarian, my wife and I. But my mother, who lives with us, thinks we are. She's much more traditional and it's important to her. So you see…" he trailed off.

June suppressed a chuckle. "I do see. Best to keep the peace."

The young man eyed the dish regretfully. "It did look very good. But we couldn't have eaten it with her in the house. She's out with my wife at the moment, but if she found it in the fridge, she might have discarded it. And as I mention, I didn't want that."

June checked her watch. In for a penny, in for a pound. If she served Dolly proscribed food, why not this nice young gentleman? "If you've got the time, why don't you stay here and we'll have it for lunch? It won't take long to heat up."

"Oh I couldn't impose. I feel bad enough as it is, rejecting your kind gesture."

June admired his slightly old-fashioned, formal turn of phrase. "It won't be an imposition."

"Then thank you. I would be very grateful." As he spoke he knocked over the tea cup, which rolled onto the floor and broke. He was horror struck, profuse with apologies and offers to recompense his hostess.

June was unperturbed. The cups were old, inherited from an aunt, but she had never greatly cared for them. The design of blue flowers with unattractive mustard-green leaves wasn't much to her taste. The tea set also hadn't been in the best condition when she had received it. The teapot had never poured well and June rarely used it. One of the cups had been chipped and another slightly cracked, and the gilt was worn on all of them. This breakage left only three in good condition.

"Not to worry at all. They're old, quite worn, and not at all of any special value. I was thinking about getting some new ones anyway," she told him. "Let's consider this a good omen."

The casserole was eaten with great appreciation. June told him about the neighbourhood, and he told her about his family. His wife was a teacher and he was an accountant, but currently taking some time off due to the move. They had relocated for work reasons. "It's hard on my mother as she had to leave all her old friends behind, but you know how it is. We offered to get her a flat there but she prefers to live with us."

After the young man left she put the remaining portion into the freezer. Before he went he had insisted that June must meet his wife and mother and dine with them later that week. June told him that she would be delighted to and reassured his anxious inquiry that she would be very happy with vegetarian cuisine.

She went out again that afternoon, back to the Red Cross shop. The rain had cleared but the sky was still leaden so she took and umbrella with her. If she took an umbrella, it wouldn't rain again. If she didn't bring one, it would. It was always the way. She had thought about taking the three unbroken cups but decided they would be more clutter than objects of desire. There was a young woman at the monthly community centre craft market who sold handmade candles made in vintage teacups. June thought she might appreciate them.

"Don't I recognise these?" Dolly asked, as she and June took tea later that evening. After indulging themselves with the Chicken à la Normande they had settled on the sofa in June's living room, watching a show they both liked. It was Stanley's evening at Rotary and he was usually back quite late. "They look very like the ones Madge Fellows had."

"They're most likely the same. I got them from the charity shop in the lower High Street," June told her. "I suspect much of Arthur's things ended up there. I thought I'd rescue them." The cups, with their pink roses on a pastel yellow background, were much prettier than Aunt Enid's had been. Yet they had held no sentimental or aesthetic value for whoever had turfed Arthur out of his home.

"Poor old Arthur. Barely past the funeral and they stuck him in that home," Dolly said. "Wicked, I call it."

June privately agreed. Though she pointed out that with his

failing sight and memory, it was unlikely Arthur Fellows could have lived by himself much longer.

Dolly shook her head. "They might have got him a carer. It's on the NHS. They come in a couple of hours a day or a few times a week, whatever's needed. And a daily woman to do his laundry and a bit of cleaning. It wouldn't have cost that much." She eyed her teacup again. "What happened to your ones?"

"Broken, mostly. I thought I'd donate the remaining ones to the craft fair."

Dolly approved. "I'll admit I never thought much of them. No point in getting too sentimental over ugly china, is there? May as well use something attractive." She took a sip of tea. "Always tastes better in a nice cup, doesn't it?"

It was a week later and when June heard an urgent knock at the door. Her doorbell was long broken - something delivery people didn't always realise - so when she heard a sharp rapping of the brass knocker she knew it was likely a friend or neighbour. And from the urgency she guessed, even before opening, that it was Dolly again.

"You've heard? Isn't it terrible? And just as I predicted," Dolly said. She had obviously come over in a rush because she hadn't bothered to pin on her favourite pearl brooch, which she rarely left the house without.

June, who had spent the afternoon reading a new cookery book from the library, had no idea what Dolly was talking about. She didn't need to inquire as Dolly kept talking.

"There was no need to move him, was there? He was perfectly alright where he was, poor old soul. And now he's gone already. Well, perhaps it's for the best. Died of a broken heart, I'd say. I'm not much of a believer but I suppose at the very least he's back with Madge, wherever she may be."

From this June discerned that Dolly was referring to Arthur Fellows. "Something's happened to Arthur?"

"Dead. Heart attack or heart failure. Or whatever they say when you're so old that nobody is particularly interested," Dolly said.

It was terribly sad. June ached for poor old Arthur, who hadn't even been able to die in the comfort of his own home.

∽

Unusual yet delicious aromas met June as she arrived at her new neighbours' home for dinner that evening. Uncertain as to whether a bottle of wine should be taken, she had instead bought flowers. She had met Mrs Gopal and her daughter-in-law Meena in the high street and was warmly greeted by them as well as Sanjay, Meena's husband.

"So glad you could come. How beautiful!" Mrs Gopal said. She was traditionally dressed in a colourful sari, while Meena wore trousers and a blouse.

Dinner, as expected, was vegetarian. June was not entirely unfamiliar with Indian food as there was a very good curry restaurant in town. But several of the side dishes and condiments were a novelty.

As they finished the main course. Meena excused herself to make a telephone call. "My pager just got buzzed. I'm not strictly on call but you know how it is."

June didn't exactly know, not being a doctor herself, but she could imagine.

"Nothing serious?" Mrs Gopal asked anxiously, when her daughter returned.

"Not this time, fortunately." Meena turned to June. "Just one of the night staff wanting to know about a medication dosage. It hasn't been the best of days. We lost a chap earlier today."

"I'm sorry to hear that," June said. "I imagine it's always hard."

"Yes. I wasn't on duty myself but the staff were very distressed. I mean with old folks it's always a possibility, but still sad. He was a lovely old chap. He didn't even get to finish his box of chocolates," Meena said. "It's the little things like that which give you a pang. He seemed so excited to receive them."

"You work with old folks?" June asked.

"Meena is one of visiting doctors for The Alders," Sanjay told her.

It was the same retirement home that old Arthur had been sent to. "It wasn't poor old Arthur Fellows that you mean, was it?" June asked.

Meena look at her in surprise. "Yes. I'm sorry if he was a friend of yours."

"He used to live a few doors down. His wife died only recently. Madge," June said. Saying the name conjured up an image of Madge. Her death had come as a surprise to everyone. She had been a few years younger than her husband. But sometimes it went that way. They hadn't had children, just nephews or second cousins or something. Relatives who never visited as far as June could recall.

Odd, perhaps, that they would have been kind enough to send a box of chocs. Guilt, June supposed. Perhaps it was Arthur's birthday. But no - that was in December or January, wasn't it? She remembered Madge having a small party for Arthur's seventieth and the Christmas decorations still being up.

Making a chicken and mushroom goulash for the family across the street, who had recently had a new baby, June felt a sense of unease. She couldn't quite put her finger on why. It was silly to be disturbed by the thought of a box of chocolates. There were any amount of reasons why they might have been sent. A neglectful relative suffering qualms of guilt. A kind person sending them to Arthur as a welcome to his new home. Someone simply misremembering his birthday.

And yet it continued to niggle at her as she diced onions and slowly stirred milk into the roux. Perhaps it was the "pang", as Meena had put it. The image of the old man, surprised and delighted, but never getting to finish his treat.

It was a mistake, of course, to tell Dolly. Dolly feasted on intrigue nearly as much as food. Combined with a vivid imagination, which she was forced to suppress around the prosaic and practical Stanley, it was a lethal combination.

"A mysterious box of chocolates! How fascinating!" Dolly exclaimed. June could almost hear the cogs whirring wickedly around in her friend's mind.

"I didn't say it was mysterious. Just unusual. I suppose I felt bad for not having visited Arthur yet myself. I meant to bring him a cake, but what with one thing and another I hadn't managed to get around to it yet. He did enjoy ginger cake, Madge made a lovely one. And now it's too late."

Dolly was perched on one of the stools in June's kitchen. She eyed the sliced mushrooms, sizzling gently in the pan with the onions. "It would be a lot easier with something homemade. Like one of your casseroles," she said.

June was nonplussed. "My casseroles?"

"You might say you'd gone mushroom picking and accidentally slipped a toadstool in. Some of the deadly ones look very like the edible ones. Act a little flustered if the police questioned you. Of course there probably wouldn't be any police, in the case of an elderly person. They'd just chalk it up to heart failure and never bother with an autopsy. Chocolates are no use, with all that cellophane."

The mushrooms had taken on a hostile appearance. Watching them wilt and brown in the pan, June found herself wishing she'd done a lemon chicken bake.

"I don't think there's any suggestion Arthur was murdered, Dolly," she said.

Dolly pressed her lips together. "Well, there wouldn't be, would there?" she said.

June had a terrible dream that night of Dolly serving a soup with fly agaric mushrooms swimming in it. "Eat up, dears," she was saying, ladling the concoction into the soup plates of her fern-patterned dining service. June wanted to cry out, to tell the other diners around the table to put their spoons down. She wasn't sure who they were. Their faces were shadowy, indistinct. But she was frozen. Immobile.

It was one of those dreams so vivid that it haunts you all the next morning. Needing a change of scene, June put on her coat and went outside. It had rained overnight and water still puddled on the pavement but the air was newly fresh and clear. Walking down the street she paused to admire the colourful bunches of flowers on display outside the corner shop. A bunch of daffodils would be just the trick to brighten her mood. Or better still, why not take a bunch to old Miss Menzies who was having her hip done this week?

"Three for two, daffs, narcissus and jonquil," the stallholder informed her, wrapping together the blooms June picked out.

Armed with a veritable floral shield reeking of spring fragrance, June set off for the hospital. Miss Menzies was a tiny, faded little spinster who had once run a sweet shop, many years ago now. Perhaps in tribute to this former profession there were several gift-boxes of chocolates by her bed, unopened. She seemed delighted by the spring flowers and even more delighted to rattle off a long list of all her various ailments.

June was a patient and practiced listener. She provided the right nods and murmurs of sympathy while her mind drifted to other matters. The ward wasn't full that day, with three empty beds between Miss Menzies' bed and the next patient, at the far end of the ward. Assuming there was a patient in it. The curtains were fully drawn around the cubicle.

Not that hospital drapes afforded much privacy, really. You could hear everything through them if you were in the next bed. June recalled overhearing an entire conversation about some poor woman's haemorrhoids and accompanying dietary guidance when she'd been in on a previous occasion.

Just as Miss Menzies was relating the latest on her rheumatism, June was startled to see two uniformed police officers enter the ward, accompanied by a nurse of senior appearance and two doctors. One of them was Meena from number five. She looked very stressed and worried.

Miss Menzies also watched the group walk brisky down the centre aisle and approach the curtained bed. "That'll be the poisoning," she informed June in a hushed whisper.

"The poisoning?"

"One of the sisters on night duty told me. Nearly died, apparently. Only a young thing too. Most probably a love affair gone wrong," Miss Menzies said.

June felt rather glad they couldn't hear what was being said, given the distance of the other cubicle. Poor young girl. They should have put her in a private room, surely?

"Back in my day they locked you up for that," Miss Menzies said. "But I didn't think they did so anymore. Can't think why they've got officers there."

Visiting hour was drawing to a close so June made motions to leave. Before she could go, one of the gift-wrapped boxes of chocolates was pressed upon her.

"Do take them, dear. Everyone brings me sweets because of the shop, but they're not at all to my taste," Miss Menzies urged. She eyed the cellophaned box with mild disdain. "In my day, of course, it was all hand-selected. Bonbons and peppermints measured from a jar, and chocolates chosen from the tray under the counter. None of this packaged stuff. Very impersonal."

There was a café adjacent to the hospital reception, a sunny room with colourful Formica-topped tables. June stopped to fortify herself with a cup of tea, putting the chocolates on the table. They weren't a favourite variety of hers or even Dolly's, despite her sweet tooth, and she wondered what to do with them.

As she sipped the tea her thoughts returned to the curtained bed. Such a sad thing, really. She'd known a woman who'd lost a daughter that way. A love affair gone wrong. The man had turned out to be married and had deserted her. A terrible waste of life. But at least they'd managed to save the patient in Miss Menzies' ward.

"Been visiting?"

June looked up to see Meena by her table.

"Just an old friend having an hip replacement," June explained. "I did see you across the ward but I didn't like to interrupt. You looked particularly occupied," she added tactfully.

Meena raised her eyebrows and sat down. "You saw the police officers?"

"I did." June didn't like to pry but it was only human nature to be curious.

"It will doubtless be all over the newspapers tomorrow."

This did surprise June. "The newspapers? For a suicide attempt?" Then she realised she probably wasn't supposed to know this. She said hurriedly: "My friend in the same ward mentioned something about it."

Meena looked grave. "It wasn't that. A poisoning. They're investigating for attempted murder."

Attempted murder? Such a thing seemed quite surreal. June wasn't really sure what to say. What could one say? "How dreadful."

"It is, yes. She was - is - the receptionist at The Alders. We've had police all over the place there since this morning."

June had vague memories of a pleasant, plump young woman with several silver rings on her fingers. She could recall the rings more vividly than the face. "Was she taken ill at work."

"No, at her home. Her flatmate fortunately called an ambulance in time," Meena informed her.

"It wasn't food poisoning?"

Meena's pager buzzed. "Unfortunately not. Cyanide." She excused herself and bustled off.

On her way out June paused by the hospital reception. "I wonder if you'd like these?" she asked, offering the box of chocolates to the woman at the desk. "My friend didn't care for them. They're unopened." They were gladly accepted and June went on her way, rather relieved to have unburdened herself of them.

"And I've never liked After Eights," Dolly announced. It was her final pronouncement on a dinner party she had attended the previous evening at the Davenports'. June had not been invited. Phyllis had never forgiven her for the rock cakes. Dolly took some loyal pleasure in detailing the deficiencies of Phyllis's menu and the inferiority of her cuisine compared to June's cooking.

"What's wrong with After Eights?" June asked.

Reaching for a biscuit, Dolly wrinkled her nose. "They're very deceptive. You always think there are plenty left but it's just the wrappers. Very disappointing."

Chocolates. Wrappers. Cellophaned boxes. Mrs Menzies' old sweet shop. Chocolates seemed to be everywhere. "I visited Elspeth Menzies earlier today," June said. She had chosen not to mention the police and what Meena had told her. It felt intrusive, somehow, to the young woman who was still gravely ill.

"How was she?"

"They're doing the hip tomorrow. She seems in good spirits. Deluged with boxes of chocolates which she was trying to give away."

Dolly gave a wry smile. "I suppose people assume she has a sweet tooth having had a confectionary shop. Did you take any?"

"I did, but I offloaded them to the receptionist. They weren't a particularly special variety."

"Hospital staff get all the chocolates and flowers left behind," Dolly said. "Never the doctors though. Or perhaps Stanley just never brought any home. I wouldn't put it past him to have kept them from me." With a triumphant gleam in her eye she took another biscuit.

True enough, as Meena had predicted, the story made the headlines of the next day's papers. "POLICE PROBE ATTEMPTED MURDER. Woman believed deliberately poisoned." Goodness only knew how journalists got hold of these things so quickly.

Naturally Dolly rushed over wielding a copy even before June had finished her morning cup of tea. "Have you heard? It's the girl at The Alders of all places. Perhaps there's a serial killer on the loose! I'll bet it's the cook. Spinach switched for rhubarb leaves. Or a toadstool casserole."

June had been thinking a lot about The Alders. Or rather dreaming about the retirement home. Images of silver rings on plump fingers had been mixed up with Miss Menzies scattering After Eight wrappers like confetti about the hospital ward. June had attributed these wild visions to a late evening snack of cheese and crackers, consumed not long before bedtime. Cheese was supposed to give you funny dreams.

"She was taken ill at her home," June told Dolly. "And it was cyanide, not whatever's in rhubarb."

This was seized on with fascination. "Cyanide?" Dolly hurriedly scanned the article again. "I don't see any mention of cyanide. Or where it happened."

"I bumped into Doctor Gopal from down the road."

As June drank her tea, from one of Madge Fellows rose-patterned cups, an idea came into her mind. It was little more than a thin crack of light around the edge of a door, but it gleamed nonetheless.

"They seem very pleasant, the Gopals. I think you mentioned they were vegetarians?" Dolly asked.

"Essentially."

"Good. I wanted to invite them all for dinner next week. You too of course. Quiche perhaps? Or a vegetarian lasagne?" Dolly nattered on about her dinner party plans while June's mind turned over the events of the past few days.

Certain things Dolly had said. Something old Miss Menzies had mentioned. A possibly very important detail that Doctor Gopal had revealed.

It might all be a mare's nest. June almost hoped it was.

At the end of the day, it boiled down to just two questions. Two simple questions. Yet June felt awkwardly foolish when she knocked at number five and the door was opened by Sanjay.

"Is your wife home? I wondered if I might ask her something. It's nothing medical but it may be rather serious," June added quickly, knowing from Dolly how doctors were plagued with ad hoc consultations in the supermarket.

Sanjay looked a little surprised but welcomed her in. His mother was delighted to see June. "Do come in and sit down. We were just about to have tea. May I pour you a cup?"

June thanked her. When they were all settled, she began. "The other evening you mentioned that Arthur Fellows - the old gentleman who died - was sent a box of chocolate. Do you remember the variety?"

Meena shook her head. "I'm afraid not. I didn't pay too much attention. I just recalled how pleased he was to have received them."

"You don't know if they were wrapped chocolates? Or if the box was wrapped?"

The doctor frowned. "You mean gift-wrapped?"

"I mean with cellophane. I'm sure it may be nothing, but I wondered... loose chocolates, you see. And unfinished, and perhaps the staff..."

"Loose chocolates?" Sanjay was also frowning.

June knew she must be sounding absurd. But she felt very flustered about it all herself. "With a cellophaned box, they can't be tampered with, you see. But if they were loose chocolates, and he ate one. And then perhaps it being an expensive brand, and the young woman didn't like to throw them away, and so..."

Toxicology tests, the tracking of a parcel, and a trial. Old Arthur Fellows may have been elderly but he had still died before his time.

An unnatural death. And very nearly a second death.

"I told you," Dolly announced as she served up slices of vegetable quiche at her dinner party. "I always said there was something fishy about his death. That's what got you thinking, June."

June was quite happy for Dolly to take credit for the detection. She still felt uncomfortable about her role in the affair even if she had been proven right.

"I always said that the easiest thing would be for June to poison one of her casseroles," Dolly continued, ignoring her husband's disapproving glance. "But injecting poison into a handmade chocolate. Nasty! And a terrible waste of good chocolates as well."

Mrs Gopal shook her head. "Greed," she said. "All to get an old man out of his house and sell it. A very great wickedness."

No one could argue with this.

"What made you suspect, June?" Sanjay asked.

June wasn't sure herself. "Many things. It just all added up. It started with a teacup, I think." The pale yellow, rose-patterned china. Madge's cherished china. So quickly and callously discarded. Just as Arthur had been.

Tomorrow, she would make another casserole. For the girl from The Alders, now home recuperating. Her ordeal was the real reason a murderer had been caught. Beef and vegetable perhaps. Or chicken and apricot? Sausage and beans. Goulash. Irish stew. Or pumpkin and lentil…

THE END

The Neurotic Nomad

Joanna Makris

I was thinking. I was thinking about peeling paint, cheap lino floors and a kitchen that had extracted itself from a 1950s TV ad.

It was a snapshot of my tiny rental apartment, and I'd spent the last half hour whining about it to my practical, go-to friend, Kara.

"Stop complaining! At least you have a view, don't you?" she asked.

"A view? All I can see is the strawberries-and-cream guy!" I snapped.

She stared at me. "Your neighbour eats British desserts?" she asked.

"No, I've told you about him. My window faces his kitchen, and he's always wearing a pair of strawberries-and-cream pyjamas when he's cooking. Whenever I look that way, I crouch as if a strawberry might disconnect itself and come hurtling towards my face."

Kara laughed. "C'mon, can't be that bad."

We were a short distance from my apartment, and Kara was itching to scrutinise my humble abode; too humble for my liking.

"It really is small," she commented, as she looked from left to right. "What are you thinking of doing?"

A fan of Rodin's works, I swivelled the chair around, and did my best imitation of his masterpiece.

But instead of setting out a strategy, my thoughts went back to a dodgy business investment that had left me short of money, and in turn led me to move into this place. It had happened over a few weeks, and my lifestyle changed faster than you can say, "I told you so."

"Are you managing okay?" Kara asked.

"Yes, as long as my rent is cheap," I said. "I should never have trusted that financial consultant with his shitty business advice."

"Don't worry about that now, focus on the future."

I tried, but kept going back to the past. I missed my art classes, where I could unleash my bursts of creativity, I missed my wine-tasting holidays, where I'd meet like-minded 'spirited' people, but mostly I missed my own space, with ample space…

My matchbox existence had forced me to quit things I loved, and I was searching for an escape, if only for the short term.

"Hey!" Kara piped up. "Why don't you try house sitting for a while? It'll be a change and you might move on to somewhere nicer for the long term."

Mmm, house sitting. Staying in other people's properties, visiting suburbs for the first time, and all for a few simple home-based jobs. It sounded great. I closed my eyes and saw myself lounging in a Spanish-style villa, a waiter serving me freshly cooked paella, and a manicurist putting the finishing touches to my Picasso-inspired toenail artwork.

I opened my eyes and came back to the present. Kara was peering at me. She always remained quiet when my imagination was running further afield.

"Consider it," she said. "Got shopping to do, catch you later."

I paced up and down my studio apartment, although four steps to the left and four steps to the right are more of a line dance than anything else.

"… move on to somewhere nicer." Kara's words echoed in my ears.

My head buzzing with excitement, I searched the internet for house sitting. The first result was an agency, and I signed up, logged out and waited for the magic to begin.

A week went by with no news. Disappointed, I put aside any potential move and went on with my life: a series of daily repetitions, with 'one step at a time' as my inspirational quote.

Each day blended into the next to complete the week. A mix of re-shuffling bills for payment, scanning the supermarket discounts and ignoring the peeling paint near the front door.

Two weeks went by. One rainy day as I was leaving the office, cursing myself for forgetting my umbrella and scuttling from awning to awning, my phone began buzzing inside my bag. I fished it out with wet hands and while trying to read a message on its raindrop-splattered screen, the phone fell into a juniper shrub. I ploughed through the slippery plant, aware of several pairs of legs just to my right.

"Need some help there?" asked one of the trousered legs.

"Oh, thanks," I replied, gripping my phone before being hoisted up by a pair of sturdy hands.

"No problem," replied a 30-something businessman. "You're lucky you didn't get your dress dirty while you were burrowing in that bush."

"Yes, thanks," I muttered, looking away from his left shoulder which now, thanks to me, was covered in soil and weeds. I squinted at my phone through the rain mist. It was a notification from the house-sitting agency.

Anxious, I gathered my bag, phone and a few tenacious juniper leaves, and rushed home to read my message. It was my first potential short-term home.

The profile pictures revealed a three-storey, seven-bedroom house with classical furniture and decorated in deep, natural colours. The time frame was ideal, as my current lease was ending soon. I made an appointment to meet Paul, the owner.

Paul lived in an affluent suburb towards the eastern part of the city, a neighbourhood with stately homes and luscious, landscaped gardens. I parked in front of his house, and through the bars of a wrought iron gate, saw a figure approaching at a leisurely pace.

"Hi, I'm Paul."

The homeowner was very welcoming, and had a kind, albeit stern face. Roughly in his mid-forties, he travelled often, and this time would be away for six weeks. He opened the gate, and we slowly strolled towards his front door. Very slowly. Paul's amble left me meditating on every step.

"There's not a lot to do, really," he said. "I want someone, ah, reliable to keep a watch over the, um, house, collect the mail, ah, contact the cleaner, and let me know if anything, um, ah, needs, ah, fixing". I waited for Paul to finish what was becoming an epic sentence. The house-sitting job sounded easy, though, and I accepted.

∽

It was surprisingly easy to move out of my studio rental. My suitcases bumped their way down the stairs and I heaved them into my car, handing the apartment keys back to my grumpy landlord. "Where ya goin'?" he quizzed.

"I don't really know," I replied, as I squeezed myself into my luggage-filled car. His sardonic expression was reflected in my rear-view mirror as I pulled out of the driveway. I left his sarcastic manner behind, casually driving over his rose bed, and could still hear him swearing as I sped down the street.

A small slice of freedom was beckoning me, and I happily headed towards it.

Paul's house was an impressive example of classic architecture. The majestic front door invited, even encouraged, a grand entrance, and I straightened my spine as I stepped over the threshold.

Once inside, though, I shrank in stature. Surrounded by space, I gazed up at the high ornate ceilings, and then towards the rear of the foyer at the marble curved staircase. One room led into another, each room showcasing intricate hand-crafted tables, classic Victorian sofas, and rare antiques. The owner had selective taste, and a preference for those dark, natural colours.

Suddenly I realised I was alone. Alone in an expanse of earthy hues: mocha, walnut brown, and the occasional sepia. I felt the sepia practically seep into my being. I walked from one end of the building to the other, hoping to find a hint of... another colour, perhaps? Flamingo pink? Even a canary yellow would've been okay.

I sat on an expensive, period chair, not really sure which period I was sitting on, and stared at a biscotti-hued wall. The wall, of course, made me hungry. Why would they name a colour after a biscuit anyway?

Navigating my way towards the kitchen, I passed through a corridor dotted with portraits of strangers. The solemn strangers glared back with disapproval, each photo duplicating the appearance of its neighbour.

The kitchen was at the end of the corridor, and on entering it I sighed with relief. It was white. In fact, ultra white. No matter, it was a change from the tan hues and had an abundant supply of biscuits.

Hunger satisfied, I came back to the magnificent, curved staircase and wandered upstairs to find my temporary lodging. It was a spacious bedroom decorated in the same sombre tints. The bed was a four-poster, a solid piece of furniture made of sturdy mahogany, with a copper-coloured duvet. Sleep came to me quickly, assisted by the gravity of my new room. I woke up the next day with a heavy head and left for work.

Arriving at my office, I felt it envelope me in a youthful spectrum of colour. It was the first time I was relieved to be surrounded by bright neon lights and indeterminate shades of blue-green.

The days progressed, and after one week at Paul's house, I felt heavier. I thought I had gained weight, but the bathroom scales disagreed. After the second week, I had a furrowed brow. And after several weeks, it was taking me longer to get from one end of the room to the other.

"Hey, I'm back! How did it go?" Paul seemed incredibly light, ethereal. Or was that my imagination? Was that a halo around his head?

"Aah... yeah... great," I croaked.

"You're a little different, more serious. And what happened to your voice?" he asked.

"The baritone, um, thing? Don't worry about it, ah, be on my way", I replied, as I shuffled past him. I wondered how long it would take to regain the spring in my step.

I always was a fast walker. Even when not in a hurry, I'm charging ahead of anyone else. My first house-sitting experience left me trudging along, and desperately trying to widen my stride.

My next house-sitting job was for a family of four who had left for their annual holiday. Their neighbour let me into their apartment, a bright, cheerful place where the sun's rays were filtering through every space.

My new room had a pleasant view, for a change, as the home overlooked a river, and I gazed at the wharf where the ferries docked. From the apartment's interior design, it was clear someone had a stylish bent. Minimalist furniture in a 'less is more' fashion, with a few decorative items. All perfectly proportioned.

Every piece of furniture was perfectly positioned at a 90-degree angle. The spaces in between appeared equidistant, as if meticulously measured. I searched for a ruler, curiosity getting the better of me, but didn't find one.

Beneath a colourful abstract work of art was a collection of family photos, strategically placed on a series of shelves. The people in the photos were smiling and attractive. Each family member had a perfectly chiselled face, as if an aerobic facial workout was part of their daily routine.

I wondered what they did. What was the father's job? Where did the mother work? Were their children good in school? Of course they were. Perfect families always have a perfect life.

The perfect couple's bedroom had soft, very soft furnishings, smooth fabrics and a room oozing with comfort. It appeared that soft and smooth had a firm place in the perfect family's lifestyle.

It was getting dark outside, and my stomach was rumbling. The fridge was stocked with fruit, vegetables, organic produce, and some vegan stuff I'd never seen before. I set to work on a salad when I detected a subtle movement, just out of the corner of my eye, something skimming across the floor.

"My imagination's playing tricks on me," I thought.

As I placed the salad bowl on the table, something flickered on the floor again. This time I caught a glimpse of a tail. I shrieked and did a sort of jig around the kitchen floor. It was a small mouse.

This was not in my plans, nor did I know how to deal with it. I was in someone else's house, and so I called the family.

"Hi there, sorry to bother you on your holiday. Quick question:

there's a small mouse in the kitchen. What can I do? Should I call pest control?"

"No, no! Don't hurt it, just ask it to leave."

"Wha... what? I think this line is really bad, I didn't hear that," I said.

"I said to just ask it to leave."

Pause.

"What do you mean exactly?" I asked.

"The same way I'm giving you instructions right now. Ask the mouse politely to go, but don't hurt it."

I love animals just as much as the next person, but I'm not sure I speak the language of mice. How do I communicate to one that it's not welcome? Besides which, it might have been there before I arrived, in which case I'm the intruder.

"Ah, sure, got it," I lied.

Not knowing where to face, as the mouse had disappeared, I stood in the middle of the kitchen and said in a loud voice, "Mouse, piss off!"

In my rashness, I'd forgotten that the owner had told me to be polite. I tried again.

"Dear mouse, please scratch my previous request. Kindly leave via any exit, and I hope your next destination will be one where you'll be staying for quite some time."

I did, for a second, question the logic in my above monologue, but I'll try anything once. After all, it might even work.

In the meantime, my stay in this home was a four-week period. Dinners in the kitchen were fast and frantic. Cooking was kept to a minimum, and eating was more of a gobble than a chew. And all to avoid another encounter with my furry flatmate.

I didn't even enjoy the perfect bedroom's soft and smooth furnishings, afraid that my flatmate would skittle in my direction in the middle of the night. Or had it confined itself to the boundaries of the kitchen?

Strangely, I never did see that mouse again, or any of its peers, bypassing the need for a rodent faceoff.

My stay in the light, breezy apartment came to an agitated end, as my stress wouldn't let me sleep, and I said goodbye to the perfect, happy family and their perfect mouse guest.

~

"Why don't you search for something more down to earth and less pretentious?" Kara asked me over a coffee. "They say that you can't judge a book by its cover."

Maybe she had a point. Why was I choosing homes based on their style, extravagance, or size? When my stay in the perfect home was coming to an end, I searched the agency's website for something different, something with more interesting content.

There it was: a simple, middle-class house. A '70s-style brick house with a small rock garden. From the website photos, it looked modest, well-kept and ordinary. Patty lived there with her pet cat. I'd be staying there for three weeks, not so much to tend to the house, but to care for Honey, the cat.

The trip to Patty's house was a more complicated venture. She lived on the outskirts of the city, and though I had the correct address, seemed to be going round in circles. The sun had well and truly set, and there was no one on the street to ask for directions. I was alone in a ghost town with the moonlight for company.

Taking a roundabout for the second (or third?) time, a tiny lane appeared in the light of the street lamp. It was Patty's street. I manoeuvred into it and parked on the corner.

"Hello, I was worried you might have trouble finding it," she said.

"Oh no, it was easy." Note to self: must stop lying.

She showed me inside her home, and it was just as she'd described it. A sensible dwelling furnished with practical, budget furniture. I glanced down at a slightly worn green rug, and guessed that would be a favourite resting spot for Honey.

"Take a seat, and I'll get Honey".

I sat on a small couch covered in a floral slipcover and was glad that I'd be staying in a simple, understated home for a while.

Patty had returned with a ginger-coloured tabby cat in her arms.

"This is Honey."

With a name like Honey, I had imagined she'd have a sweet temperament. I was searching for a hint of sweetness, but was greeted by a steely-eyed kitty.

"I'll be off," said Patty, leaving me alone with her cat.

"Hi there, Honey." Honey looked up at me from the floor, piercing me with her gaze and spiking my soul.

"Let's get to know each other," I said. Honey jumped onto the couch and curled up next to me. "There's the sweetness," I thought.

I stroked her back. She got up and changed position, her twitching tail facing me. What did that mean? Did she want more stroking? Or none at all? I stroked her back a little more. She jerked to one side, and with a vicious swipe, scratched my hand before settling back into resting mode.

Nursing my scratches and my wounded pride, I left the couch to prepare her dinner. Everything was in the pantry on the third shelf: cat food, cat toys, cat brush, cat bowl, and all neatly labelled.

"Honey, time to eat!" I called, hoping she would warm to me with the promise of a tasty meal. She was staring at her bowl, and occasionally threw a furtive glance in my direction.

I took a step forward to add food into her bowl when she suddenly froze. With back arched, her legs now resembled four pillars with dagger-like claws, and her tail had transformed itself into a weight-bearing weapon. Her iron-clad eyes drilled right through me.

"Okay, Honey, I'll leave you alone."

Making my way back to the couch, I heard a low growl. I spun on my heels, worried that Honey was choking on her food, and saw her in mid-flight. She had sprung off the floor and was aiming for my chest. Her legs had become metallic rods as she landed on my torso, embedding her claws into my arms and waist.

I screamed a loud, shrill sound, several octaves higher than I thought was humanly possible. A petrified cat was attached to me, and if it wasn't for the immense pain I felt, I would have laughed at the sight of myself in the mirror. Honey had fastened her claws into my skin, and the expression on my face was ghastly.

I've never really danced rock and roll, but suddenly found myself swinging around the living room floor on fast forward with

Honey as an unlikely partner. Tired, Honey eventually released her hold and leapt to the floor. Her hunger got the better of her, and now ignoring me, she enjoyed her dinner.

The days that followed were a mix of pushing Honey's bowl towards her with a broomstick, tending to my battle scratches, and generally remaining invisible in Honey's world. Her warlike stance was odd, as cats were usually fond of me.

Patty's return was a relief. She was confused at my attempt to make a speedy exit, and asked why there was so much antiseptic in the bathroom.

"Oh, I fell over and used it for some scratches," I lied yet again, unable to describe my prickly encounter with Honey.

"Well, I'm glad I'm back. My divorce is final," Patty confided to me. "He made things difficult, but it's all worked out well now. He was pure evil. Look, I've still got a small picture of him. Doesn't he have the face of a demon?"

I peered at the small, worn photo she placed in my hand. The man in the photo was gorgeous, but he did have a satanic grin. What did his eyes remind me of? A furtive squint? A steely-eyed gleam?

Leaving the house, I caught a glimpse of Honey's sideways glance. Was that a steely-eyed expression of glee? I drove away faster than I've ever driven, haunted by Honey's eerie impersonation of her previous owner.

They say, 'third time lucky'. In that case, it would seem that my luck had run out. The house-sitting jobs had also run out.

"How did you get yourself into this?" Kara, forever pragmatic, asked me a question I'd already asked myself.

"Didn't you search for another home before you finished up at the last one?" she continued, unable to understand my reasoning.

"Yes, no, I mean there aren't always places available," I replied, unable to explain my reasoning, or the lack of it.

"You can stay at my place as long as you need, but you should decide what you really want to do," she offered.

In my rush to start a house-hopping adventure, I hadn't thought about long-term accommodation. With over three months of living like a nomad, I had no concrete idea of where I was going, or what type of place I wanted to house sit.

For a second, I missed my former rented apartment, but shot down that idea before it took form.

∽

My phone buzzed. New notification, and another. I was becoming popular on the house-sitting site, but wasn't ready for another misadventure.

"More notifications?" Kara asked.

"They just keep coming in. I'm not sure what to do."

We were having lunch at the Italian café, a cosy restaurant with red and white checked tablecloths. As I munched on my capricciosa salad, I could smell the scent of fennel from my plate. It reminded me of liquorice, and took me back to my childhood when I used to stuff it in my pockets thinking no one had noticed.

"Why are you tossing the salad with your nose?" Kara asked.

I landed in the present. "Oh, I like the fennel. It reminds me of my childhood."

"Come back to adulthood. What are you planning for your next move?" she asked.

Ah, planning. Not my strongest attribute. Future planning, at least. I shifted in my chair, and went into my habitual chin-on-the-fist, elbow-on-the-knee position.

"Hey, 'Thinker', let's go." Kara was losing her patience.

Kara went to the bus stop, and I went for a walk around her neighbourhood; a suburb with older and newer houses, with patios and porches, and freshly mowed lawns. A wide, tree-lined road led me to a real estate agency, and I browsed the property rentals in the window.

"Hi there, can I help you?" The question was asked by a tall man with a warm smile, dressed in a navy suit, and standing just inside the door.

"I'm not sure yet," I replied. "I'm getting an idea of what's around."

There was something comfortable about him, a sense of familiarity, but I couldn't put my finger on it.

"Are you searching specifically in this suburb?" he asked.

"This area certainly is vibrant," I replied, "but I'm not sure yet."

"Well, it is a lovely part of the city. Take your time and look around the neighbourhood. Come in, and let me give you my business card." He retreated into the agency with long strides, and disappeared into a small room to the right of the entrance.

I stepped inside the agency and waited in the foyer. A young couple also walked in, and as I moved aside, the real estate agent popped out of the small room, colliding with me, and dropping his card onto my breasts. It became lodged between my dress and bra, like a small flag with printed instructions for onlookers.

All eyes were on me, or rather on my breasts. I pretended that was the most logical place for the card to be, and continued the small talk, aware that the card was shifting position each time I inhaled or exhaled.

Blushing slightly, the real estate agent greeted the couple, and turning back to me said, "Call any time, I'd be happy to help you find your dream place." His eyes met mine, and again I had that familiar feeling about him.

"Thanks, I'll probably contact you again soon," I stuttered. His card was still on my breasts. I turned abruptly, hoping the card would follow, but it fell to the floor.

"Oh, there it is!" I announced, as I picked it up and swiped it through the air for everyone to see. Transferring the card to my pocket and with a hasty goodbye, I set off for Kara's home.

My head was crowded with infinite thoughts, and my beloved Thinker pose wouldn't make a difference. I pondered on my next house move, Kara's impatience and the strange, almost intimate encounter with the real estate agent.

My phone buzzed. Another notification. One house-sitting message after another, and I pored through them, dissecting each home in a search for potential flaws.

Too dark, too light, two cats. None of them impressed me.

I put my phone on silent and walked up the stairs to Kara's place.

~

Kara's home was a tranquil respite. I'd been staying there for about three weeks and was getting used to its quiet predictability. She loved nature and had filled her living room with plants of various types, mostly fern and ivy, creating a warm and comforting atmosphere.

From her apartment, I caught a different bus to get to my office, one of the many bus routes I'd used in the last four months.

"Have you moved?" asked Jen, forever inquisitive, who was working with me on a team project. "I saw you on my bus this morning on my way to the office. Don't you normally come from another direction?" she added.

"I'm staying with a friend. I've also been house sitting at various places for about four months," I managed to confess.

"Oh, that's exciting!" Jen was beside herself. "How was that?"

My reply was an expressionless glare, with a slight twitch developing in my left eye.

Jen looked unsettled. I attempted to make conversation.

"It was cool," I quipped. I was standing in front of the small water fountain, then moved behind it, creating a barrier of water droplets between us.

Jen narrowed her eyes and stared at me through the cascading water. "Are you all right?" she asked.

"Sure. Just wanted to see how you'd look in the shower."

She widened her eyes. By avoiding house-sitting talk, I'd thrown my sexual orientation into a cloud of confusion.

I wasn't even sure why I reacted that way. My recent 'housecapades' must have dislodged my neatly compartmentalised mind.

I went back to the team project, hoping that would have a calming effect.

~

The project did relax me. Conversation had stopped, and I didn't have to explain why I was living out of a suitcase. In fact, work was going well. It was the one good thing going on in my life.

It was five minutes to six. I stopped reading the weekly report and closed my eyes to meditate for a few minutes, hoping that would prompt my mind out of the recent mad chaos, and lead it into a kind of organised one.

I opened my eyes, and dialled the real estate agent's number, expecting no answer at such a late time.

"Hello?"

"Oh hi! I wasn't sure anyone would be there," I said.

"Yes, working a bit late tonight," he replied.

"I don't know if you remember me, I'm..."

"I remember you, I remember your voice," he sweetly interrupted. I could feel a warmth trickling through my veins.

"Oh, okay. Well, I want to make an appointment to talk about sales, not rentals," I said decisively. "And I am interested in that neighbourhood."

We met at the Italian café. He was sitting at the corner table and smiled when he saw me.

I weaved my way through the tables towards him, glancing at the red and white checked tablecloth framing his waist. Not so much red, more of a pinky-red, a shade that jolted my memory.

"Hey, how was your day?" he asked.

"Good. Finished some long-standing matters today," I replied, losing my train of thought.

I sat down opposite him. The tables at the café were compact, and I could examine his face in more detail. His eyes were a tawny colour, a tantalising hue, reminding me of a tiger-print scarf I once had. Or did they remind me of a tiger, minus the scarf? Almost hypnotic, his eyes never left mine. I studied his lean face, and as my eyes had taken on special powers, they could see right through his shirt.

The energy shifted when our coffees arrived and, remembering the purpose of our meeting, we settled into subdued business chat. We talked about apartment sales, government grants, mortgages, renovations. With my confidence returning, I started making mental calculations on property purchases and mortgage payments.

The atmosphere changed again, our senses heightened once more.

"Would you like to go for a walk in my neighbourhood?" he asked. "I live in a suburb close to the real estate agency."

"Yes."

We walked towards his part of the city and as we approached his street, the surroundings were very familiar. We arrived in front of his building and I stared in disbelief.

"You won't believe this, but I used to live in the building right next door!" I exclaimed.

He just smiled, and invited me in.

He lived on the third floor of a modern, newly built apartment block. Home was a large apartment designed in the Hamptons style: white with grey-blue accents and slim-line furniture.

The living room and kitchen were open plan, and I spotted a stained-glass window above the kitchen sink, a creative touch to a modern home.

"Would you like a glass of red? Or if you prefer white wine?" he asked.

"Red."

I watched him pour the wine, running my eyes along the length of his arm towards his shoulder. Just past his shoulder, a part of his bedroom was visible. There was a print on the wall above his bed; a print of Rodin's sculpture, 'The Kiss'.

"You like Rodin?" I asked, the back of my neck tingling.

"Yes, that's a print of 'The Kiss', my favourite art piece."

His favourite art piece, by Rodin. A ripple of optimism passed through my body, helped by the effects of the wine.

I put my glass on the sideboard and sauntered into the bedroom to inspect the print. He followed, and as I turned, our eyes locked once more.

His tiger eyes had specks of gold, and I took step closer.

I faltered; I knew nothing about him. Yet we had a mysterious connection, and I gained momentum once more.

As I drew closer, my peripheral vision was obscured by a pinky-red object. It prodded my memory, and its intrusion made my mood wax and wane. Curious, I pivoted a fraction towards the door.

Draped over a chair was a pair of pyjamas, featuring rows of strawberries in a sea of frothy cream.

"You - you're the strawberry guy?" I blurted out.

He smiled. "You didn't realise?" he asked. "I was sure you knew."

What I did know, was that passion and nausea could not co-exist in my psyche.

I glared at the pyjamas. The strawberries seemed to be mocking me, as they claimed their corner of the bedroom.

Something inside me snapped.

"Hey!" I said. "Throw your pyjamas out of the window."

"What?"

"The pyjamas, throw them out of the window!"

"Why? I thought you found them fun?" he asked. "I could see you through my kitchen window."

He got that from my facial contortions?

"Besides," he said, "I like the pyjamas."

He liked the pyjamas. This required a more complex strategy. I decided to negotiate.

"I'll buy you another pair with any other fruit you want."

He smiled, and the strawberry pyjamas went flying out of the window. And with a little luck, possibly landing on my ex-landlord's head.

"Now," I said. "Where were we?"

Two years later, we're still together.

He wears orange-and-mandarin pyjamas. I'm okay with the citrus thing.

But strawberries, those we never touch…

THE END

The Rings

Conchita GarSantiago

Plain white walls surrounded the simple bed where a monitor was attached to her arm. Faint heartbeats could be heard.

'I'm sorry Mr Williams,' the doctor said softly 'I wish we could do more for your wife, but I'm afraid it's just a matter of hours. Maybe days.'

Tears fell down his old dark cheeks and he covered his face with his right hand, while his left held on tightly to Tracy's hand. His long skinny black fingers intertwined with her shorter chubby white fingers, all covered with thick gold rings.

An elegant, slim lady with green eyes walked in, 'How is she?'

Malcolm, Mr Williams, looked back to see his step-daughter, Kim. He shook his head. Kim passed her hands over Malcolm's shoulders. 'I heard what the doctor said.' She sobbed. 'We knew Mum's in her last days.'

Kim sat with her stepfather, holding hands with him and sobbing in silence. After twenty minutes, she said, 'I need to go to the shop. My assistant has to leave now.'

'You go, darling.'

They kissed and then she kissed her mother. 'I just need to be there for an hour or so, until Brenda comes to replace me. But you know Brenda is new and I can't leave her alone for a long time.'

'Don't worry about coming back.'

'No. I want to. I want to be here as much as I can. As the doctor said, it's not going to be long. So… I'll come even if it's only for ten minutes.'

'As you wish.'

Malcolm watched Kim leave, still holding his wife's hands and sobbing. He couldn't imagine life without his darling Tracy.

The nurse bustled in to do another round of checks.

'Her hands are swelling.' She observed. 'Maybe we should remove those rings from her hands, before it's too late.'

'Yes. I think we should do that. I'm sure Kim would like to keep her mother's rings.'

'Yes, I agree. They are very big and she's got more than one in each finger. Your daughter will have a good memory from her mother.'

'She's not my daughter. When I married Tracy, she was already forty and Kim was seven.' He looked at her trying not to let more tears out. 'We've been married for twenty-five years. Twenty five glorious years.' He sobbed. 'She had these rings when I met her and she has never removed them.'

The nurse went ahead with the task. 'Oh look, she's got a tattoo on her little finger.' the nurse said, busying herself with removing the other rings. As she did so with each finger, a tattoo was revealed.

'They look like words.' The nurse said once Tracy's fingers were naked.

'I can't make out what it says.' Malcolm was trying to read.

'They've obviously been there for a long time.'

'As I said, I never saw her remove these rings.'

The nurse eventually made out what each word read, from each of Tracy's fingers. 'Beg for your...' She read the rest in silence and straightening up she looked at Malcolm not very sure what to say or do.

'What?' The nurse remained quiet and a flush of embarrassment crossed her face, Malcolm put on his reading glasses and holding both of Tracy's hands he read. 'Beg for your meagre life you fucking nig..ers.'

A cold chill ran through his body. He dropped Tracy's hands and stood up. He felt dizzy.

He looked at his own hands as if he needed to reaffirm they were black. He was a black man, married to that white woman. A woman he thought he knew. Did he? Tracy's whole body disappeared to Malcolm's eyes. He could only see her fingers. Those fingers with those words couldn't belong to his darling Tracy. His head spun. About to faint, he held himself on to the bars of the bed and wobbling, he headed for the door.

∼

'Malcolm! What happened? What are you doing? Why aren't you with Mum?' Kim had entered her mother's flat and was trying to get some explanations from Malcolm who was silently sitting by the window. He looked at her and then he looked back to the window.

'I know that this must be very difficult for you,' Kim sympathised with Malcolm, 'but you need to pull yourself together. There's not much time. She'll be gone any moment. Come on, let's go!' She was talking in haste.

Malcolm's voice was calmer. 'Did the nurse give you your mother's rings?'

Kim was confused by the question. 'Yeah... Come on, I'll be in the car waiting for you.' She was leaving.

'I'm not coming!'

'What?'

'Did the nurse tell you anything when she gave you the rings?'

'What?' She was more confused. 'No! Who cares about the rings? Le...'

'I do!' Malcolm yelled.

'You want the rings? I can give you the rings!'

'No! I don't want the fucking rings!'

Confused and scared, Kim slammed the door as she left. "I don't care how sad he is, he's not talking to me like that." She thought as she went down the stairs.

Back at the hospital, she found the nurse who was attending to her mother. 'Excuse me. Sorry, this morning when you gave me the rings I didn't have time to talk.'

'Don't worry about it.' The nurse stared at her and hesitated. 'Did you speak to your step-father?'

'Well, I spoke and he yelled.' There was a moment of silence. 'What's going on? He said something about the rings.'

'Did you see your mother's hands?'

'What? I... I just saw her briefly this morning, when you gave me the rings. Then I left. As I told you, I was in a hurry.'

'Come with me.'

The two ladies approached the bed where Tracy was lying. Her hands were inside the blankets. The nurse took them out. 'Read what it says.'

Kim clasped her mother's hands, read "the message" and gasped.'How could that be? She's married to a black man!'

'I'm sorry. I don't know what to tell you.'

Alone, Kim sat next to her mother. 'Mum. Please wake up. Wake up even just for five minutes to explain this.' Tracy moved her head. For a moment Kim thought she was going to start to speak but she didn't.

Kim sat in silence by her mother's bed, sad and confused.

She held and kissed her hands.

Those hands that has given her so much protection and love.

Those hands that guided her when she walked to school for the very first time.

Those hands that caressed her before falling sleep in the darkness.

Those hands that dried her eyes when they were crying and combed her hair when she needed to be beautiful.

Those hands could not have been hiding that atrocious message.

Kim called her step-father. Malcolm was still sitting by the window. When the phone rang, he looked at it, but didn't move. The machine answered and he heard Kim talking.

'Malcolm. Please answer the phone. I know you're there.' She sighed 'Look. I know why you're upset and I understand. I promise I do. I am as confused as you are, but... Mum just died.' Malcolm shook his head and looked down, but again he remained indifferent. 'You should come, otherwise, you will regret it for the rest of your life.' She was going to hang up, but then she spoke again. 'You knew her. She was loving and caring and she loved you very much. There must be an explanation for this.'

The day of the funeral was very grey. Suddenly some very dark clouds discharged a pelting rain. The large crowd attending opened their black umbrellas. Kim was trying to see Malcolm, but he wasn't there.

∽

Kim crossed the busy road and walked a short distance along the footpath until she arrived at her shop. She lifted the metal net gate that protected the shop and its contents and went inside leaving her keys and handbag on the counter. She switched on all the bright lights and started to "dress" the windows with beautiful expensive jewellery on dark red velvet boxes.

She always started with the big necklaces, followed by watches and bracelets, pendants with their chains and finally earrings and rings.

Rings... they had a different meaning than they had four months ago, when her mother passed away.

Every time she put a ring on a lady's finger to show her how it looked, and removed the ring again, she could see those frightful tattoos. Rings weren't beautiful pieces of jewellery anymore. They were sinister objects that hid obnoxious secrets.

She put them all on sale promising herself she wouldn't buy new ones.

She understood that if it made that impression on her, it would be much worse for her step-father. Malcolm... They hadn't seen each other since that frightful moment. Should she call him?

Her thoughts went to her mother, the many times she'd been with her in the shop looking at earrings, necklaces or bracelets, but never at rings. She remembered the occasional time when she said, 'Mum, you have had those rings for years, why don't you change them?'

'I like these ones. They've been with me almost all my life and I don't want to change them.'

'Well, at least let me clean them.'

'Leave them there. They'll come with me to the grave.'

'They'll come with me to the grave.' Her mind echoed the last sentence. "She was telling me not to remove those rings and I never realised!" She passed the cloth over the counter window. "She wanted her secret to go to the other world with her." Her hands were moving things on the counter to give it a good clean, but her mind was still fixated on the rings. The tattoos. "Now that the secret is out, I have to get to the bottom of the matter."

∼

As soon as the last client left her shop, Kim closed for the day. It was already five thirty and the city was starting to wind down.

She walked along the familiar streets of Sydney.

The entrance of the building was dark and the paint of the walls was crumbling. Inside was no better. Faded paint and cheap doors. She knocked on number 8.

'Come in.'

'Mr Benietti,' Kim said as she entered. 'We spoke on the phone. My name is Kim.' A man in his forties was sitting on a chair behind a desk with towers of papers on it and food wrappers spread out over his desk. By the bin, there were a few empty beer bottles.

A feeling of going back in time invaded Kim. The room looked like the ones in the private investigators' movies from the fifties.

'Oh. Yes. Your mother is the one with the rings and the tattoos.' Benietti's voice made Kim snap out of her thoughts. '…And you want me to investigate why she had the tattoos.'

'Right.'

'Did you bring the rings?'

'Yes.' She put them on the table.

'Well, you said you are a jeweller. Do you know if any of these rings are special?'

'Special?'

'Odd. Some… making marks.' Kim looked blank. 'I mean, costume made.'

'I don't think so.' She picked up some of them. 'They are old… this one has a more peculiar design, but apart from being old… I don't think you'd find…' She stopped. 'Well, here they are if you want to track them.'

Mr Benietti took a wedding ring and looked at it with his magnifier. 'There's a name here.'

'Excuse me?'

'In this wedding ring. You never noticed it?'

'To be honest, I saw them all together on my mother's fingers and I never realised it was a wedding ring. When the nurse gave them to me in the hospital, I just put them inside my bag without looking at them and they've been there until today.'

'Does the name Andrew Patterson mean anything?'

'No.'

'What about the date; 29 May, 85?'

'That's the day Mum got married.'

'To Andrew Patterson.'

'No, to Andrew Kenneth. My father.'

Benietti looked at her. After a while, he spoke. 'Well, still it's a good clue.' Then he added. 'May I have a picture of him?'

'I don't have any. Mum said that she lost a suitcase on her way here and all the pictures were there.'

'Where did they get married?'

'In England.'

'Where exactly?'

'I don't know. I was born in London. After my father died, we came to Australia.'

Mr Benietti was pensive. 'What about your grandparents?'

'All dead.'

'What about your mother's maiden name?'

'Brown.'

'You think you could find any picture from your time in England?'

'I don't think so, but I'll check.'

On the way home, Kim remembered her mother gave her a box saying, "in case I die". Kim had never looked at it. But now was the moment.

As soon as she arrived home, she looked for the box. Among the papers inside, she found her birth certificate. Kim was single and had never left Australia. She had never had a need for her birth certificate. She put her hand on her mouth as she read it. Her father was Andrew Ian Patterson and her mother Tracy Mary Morley. Her full name was there as well. Kimberly Grace Patterson. How did her mother manage to fool the school's administration? Her papers had always said, Kim Kenneth. She probably told them as well that she lost her suitcase. She was going to call the private investigator, when she saw a picture. It was a very bad photo where you could see people in the distance in front of a building. She grabbed everything and decided to go to his office instead of calling.

'I think this photo must have some meaning. Otherwise, why would it be there?'

'Let me see.' He took his magnifier. 'The phone booths in here look British. Did your mother ever mention any place in England?'

'Yes! Now I remember! Ealing!'

'Let's check in Google maps.'

Benietti keyed in the word Ealing and then with the help of Google view, it was as if they were walking along the main streets of Ealing. Then, they saw the building that was in the picture.

'This is a council. People get married here.' Mr Benietti took the picture again and picking up his magnifier said. 'You see? Your mother has a bunch of flowers. You can bet they were married here.'

He put everything down on the table and linked his hands in front of his face.

'If you want me to continue with this investigation, I have to go to England.'

'I was afraid you'd say that.'

'Obviously, it will be... expensive.'

'Couldn't you start some investigation here and if you need it...'

'I'm going to need it. The answer you want is in London, before your mother came here.'

'Mum had some friends here. They might know something.'

'Ok. Give me names and addresses and I'll visit them.'

Kim thought again. 'No.'

'No?'

'Sorry. I need some time to think how I want to proceed.'

She took all the rings, papers and the picture and left.

As she was leaving the building, she thought to herself, she didn't need him. She would do the investigation on her own.

It'll be good to have something different to do. She could close the shop for a couple of months. All optimistic, she thought, "Melissa was a good friend of Mum. She might know something I don't know."

∼

Melissa was short and overweight. Her blue eyes and round face gave her a look of sweetness. She was, after all, a sweet and kind lady. 'I've cried a lot for your mother, you know? She was too young to die.'

'Yes. Thank you.'

'I told my friend, Louise, that I'm so very sad for Mrs Malcolm.'

"Funny," Kim thought, "Mum made up a maiden last name and a married last name, and the one she didn't take, Malcolm's last name, is how people knew her here."

'You've known her since she came to this country.' Kim started to speak. 'Did Mum tell you anything about the time she was in England?'

'Only that she lived in Ealing.'

'Nothing about my father?'

'No. Not your father nor your grandparents. She said they were all dead.' Melissa sat. 'Poor woman. I've got the impression she had a tough life before coming here.'

'Well, my father was quite rich. That should have given her a comfortable life.'

'I don't know. She never wanted to talk about him. It pained her!'

'Did she ever tell you anything about the accident?'

'The accident?'

'Yes. The accident... when my father died. She mentioned a few times "the accident" but she never explained it.' In a softer voice, she added, 'not to me, anyway.'

Melisa's look was lost in thought. 'No. Neither to me.'

After one hour of conversation and tea, Kim didn't know anything she hadn't known before.

As she left Melissa's home, she was thinking, "Five names. Five. Mrs Williams, Mrs Kenneth, Mrs Patterson, Miss Brown and Miss Morley. Well, only Kenneth and Brown were made up." She voiced her thoughts, softly. 'Why Mum?' A few moments later, she voiced them again looking at the sky, 'What did you have to hide?' and the one she didn't dare to give voice to was, "why did you have those words tattooed on your fingers?"

Kim visited more of her mother's friends, but nobody said anything different to what Melissa had said.

She prepared for her trip to London.

The Captain announced they were approaching London. Window' blinds were put up and bright light came into the cabin.

'Well, this isn't the London everybody talks about, raining and grey.' Beaming, Kim commented to her neighbour.

The sign of fasten seatbelts flashed on and they started the descent into London Heathrow.

As they dived into a thick dark cloud and eventually came out under it, the grey didn't disappear.

'What did you say about London not being as grey as people say?' her flying companion asked sarcastically.

'Bummer.'

Hours later, she was standing in front of Ealing Council. She looked around as if wanting to find ghosts. Realising she wasn't going to find anything useful, she went to the registry office.

In the books she found: Andrew Ian Patterson Married to Tracy Mary Morley on 29th of May 1985 at Ealing Council.

She went to the desk. 'May I see the book for deaths in Ealing in the year, 1990?'

There he was. Andrew Ian Patterson. Her heart went to her

throat when she saw "cause of death, murdered". With a pounding heart, she quickly closed the big brown, hardcover book. It slammed with a thunk.

Her heart and her nerves needed a break. Not to mention the jet lag that she was starting to feel. Having a sensation she was going to faint, she took a taxi and went to her hotel in the Hill of Richmond.

She had a shower and went downstairs to the dining room.

Stepping shyly into it, she took a moment to observe her surroundings. The room was spacious with many tables, but not crowded. The furniture was French style and above them, large chandeliers with their shining crystals were softly dancing in the wind that was coming through one of the open windows. Two of the walls had big windows, framed with European golden and green Jacquard curtains fully opened with a great view of the descent of the hill and a curve of the Thames just before arriving at Richmond Bridge.

The clouds slightly lifted and allowed some sun's rays to come through.

'Beautiful,' she said in a low voice.

A waiter showed her to a table and gave her the menu. She wasn't very hungry. Just as well because, the French chef offered a menu of modern cuisine that meant small portions. She ordered a traditionally smoked Scottish salmon and English asparagus.

Back in her room, she started to write in her book her only, but astonishing discovery. "Well, I suppose my next move should be to the police station. If Dad was murdered, the police must know something." With that thought, she left the book on the bedside table and fell asleep.

The Bobby was a big man with a big belly and round face. He had a little moustache which made his face look short of comical.

His uniform was too tight and the brass buttons looked like they were going to shoot out of the uniform.

'I'm sorry madam, but the files are classified.'

'Look, we're talking about my father. You see?' Kim showed the man her birth certificate. 'I've got the right to know what happened to my father.'

The constable was a kind man and felt pity for her.

'Alright. As you're technically next-of-kin, I'll let you see the file.' He returned to where she was standing, with a paper folder. 'You said, Andrew Ian Patterson, dead in 1990?'

'Yes.'

'Here he is. He was stabbed to death.' Kim looked at him and then at the papers. 'You didn't discover who murdered him?'

'His wife was the main suspect, but we couldn't prove it.' Kim stepped back until her legs found a chair. She sat down and put her head in between her legs.

After puffing out breath a few times, Kim, with a slight hope that it wasn't her mother and, hoping against hope that her father had remarried, asked, 'could you please tell me the name of his wife?'

'Tracy Mary Morley. Born in 1953. 13th May.'

Kim ran to the ladies and threw up. Then, she bent over the sink and splashed her face with cold water. No matter how much water she splashed, the nightmare didn't go away. How could it be possible they suspect her mother of a murder. Her mother murdering her father? Impossible! They had it all wrong!

When she came out, the policeman was outside the door.

'Here. Have a drink,' he said handing her a glass of water.

'Thank you.'

'Are you feeling better?'

'My mother was not a murderer. She could never hurt someone.' She stretched and breathed deeply 'how did my father die?'

'I told you. A knife straight to the heart.'

'My mother didn't do that.' Kim looked down. 'Do you have any other information about my mother?'

'Well, not much.' The policeman was browsing through the file. 'Daughter of Thomas and Gladys Morley.'

A thought ran through her head. "Was it possible that Mum hasn't been honest about her parents being dead?" Her voice was soft and shameful as she asked, 'Are they still alive?'

'Let me see.' The policeman consulted his computer. 'Mr Morley, Thomas Morley had a traffic fine two weeks ago.'

Kim put her hand on her forehead while she shook her head.

The policeman carried on shuffling through papers. 'Oh yeah. We have Mrs Morley as well. They don't live together.' He looked at Kim. 'We had to go to her residence because of some altercation with her neighbours.'

'What about Andrew Patterson's parents?'

'Both dead.' The policeman looked at Kim, doubtfully.

'What?'

'Their death was suspicious, as well.'

'Excuse me?'

'The two of them died within a few days of each other and the medical examiner couldn't give a clear reason.'

Kim looked at the man with a perplexed face.

'It says here, it could be poison.'

'Could be?'

'Well, your grandfather died first and it says natural causes. But then, when your grandmother passed away so soon after him, they suspected it wasn't a coincidence. They wanted to exhume his body, but his son had ordered a cremation.'

'How could they not be sure?'

'In 1981, when they died, labs didn't have as many resources as they do today. There are a few poisons that can disappear from the body within a few hours.'

'I think I need to go.'

Back in her room, she felt defeated by her emotions. She lay in bed, although it didn't make her feel better.

The following day, however, she felt a renewed energy. She typed in a Google search for the white pages for London and found her grandparents' addresses.

The stone paved tidy street was extremely narrow. Its terrace houses, facing so close to each other, although two storeys, hardly stood twelve feet from the ground.

"I think this is it." Kim stood in front of number 7. Her heart was beating fast as she softly knocked on the door. A very old lady walking with a frame, came to open it.

'Are you my...' She stopped herself. 'Mrs Morley?'

'Who?'

Kim raised her voice. 'Are you Mrs Morley? Mrs Thomas Morley?'

The old woman looked at her with contempt.

'I checked in the white pages. Mrs Gladys Morley lives in this street, number 7'

'No.' As she was going to slam the door, Kim put her hand on it. 'Please, Mrs Morley give me a minute. Just... a few questions? Please!'

The woman was going to close the door and Kim took a fifty pound note and waved it at her. She went to grab it. 'First, answer my questions.' Kim's voice was assertive.

'What do you want to know?'

'Can I come in?' The old woman released the door and started to walk inside.

Kim followed Mrs Morley along the short low ceiling corridor, towards her small living room. There was a two-seater sofa, one armchair and a tiny low round table in the middle. In the corner, opposite to the armchair, was another table where the TV sat. The room was very dark. Mrs Morley sat on the armchair. The sofa was full of dirty cushions, blankets and newspapers. Kim looked around not sure what to do, then, carefully she picked up the blankets and put them on the back of the sofa and then the newspapers on the floor.

'Mrs Morley, you and Mr Morley had a daughter.'

'Maybe.'

Kim was losing her patience. 'A daughter called Tracy.' The old woman didn't say anything, so she carried on talking. 'Your daughter was born on the 13th of May 1953.'

'That little brat!' She spat on the floor.

'Why was she a brat?' Kim's voice came out calmer than she felt.

'A fucking princess!' Then with a mocking voice, she added, 'her and her daddy.'

Kim looked at this woman, her grandmother. She didn't look at all like her mother. Her face features weren't similar and her countenance was all the opposite. Tracy had an amiable face. This woman sitting in front of her, looked like she was going to attack at any moment. 'Aren't you interested to know what happened to her?'

'Not really.'

'She died and left some money.' Kim said with acrimony.

'Well, how much did she leave?'

'Agghh.' Kim stood up and started to walk away. Then she sat again. 'Will you, please answer my questions?' Trying to calm herself she carried on. 'When she was little... what type of friends did she have?'

'Friends.'

'Were they... British?'

'Of course, they were British. We live in Britain.'

'Were they... black?'

'I don't know.' She looked at the window. 'I don't think so.'

'Do you remember any of her friends that are still around?'

'Nah.'

'What about Mr. Morley. Is he around?'

'No. He's not.'

'You don't know anything about your husband?'

'No. I don't. Why would I need to know?'

Kim threw the fifty pounds to Mrs Morley and she stood up to leave.

'What about the inheritance?' Mrs Morley asked in a loud voice.

She came back to the little room. 'Aren't you sad that your daughter died?' The old woman got up. Kim was fuming.

'Well, yes. I'm very sad.' Mrs Morley didn't show any sad feelings.

'I see how sad you are, but you see, Tracy had a daughter and she is very sad, so the inheritance goes to her.'

Kim started to walk out and the old woman followed her. She was going to slam the door on Kim, but she stopped it. 'Aren't you interested in knowing who your granddaughter is?'

Mrs Morley didn't say a thing. 'It's me!' Kim yelled. 'But don't expect me to call you grandmother.'

∼

Riding in the tube to go to see Mr Morley, she was sad. "How can that woman be my mother's mother? Mum was kind, caring, loving..."

Her heart was telling her to stop the investigation and go home. Her head was telling her she had to keep going.

When she arrived at Mr Morley's house, Kim was feeling sick. "I don't think I can do this." She started to walk away, but she came back. "I have to do it! If I don't see him, I'll regret it for the rest of my life."

She rang the bell. A tall man well dressed and with a pleasant face opened the door.

'Mr Morley? Thomas Morley?'

'Yes. How can I help you?' Kim was relieved to see her grandfather had a more affable attitude.

'I'd like to ask you some questions about your daughter. Tracy.'

'Who are you?'

'I'm... a private investigator...'

The face of the old man was a mixture of sadness and excitement. 'Did my daughter hire you?'

Kim realised he was taking false hope.

'I'm sorry. Your daughter is dead.'

A few tears ran down the old man's face. After a few moments of silence, he moved, letting her come in.

'I haven't seen my daughter for many years. All I knew was that she went to Australia.' He sat on an armchair and gestured to his visitors to sit in front of him. 'I think she had a family.'

The house was bigger than Mrs Morley's and the living room was very comfortable and bright.

'How did you know she was in Australia?'

'A friend of hers told me.' He said. Then, he added with exasperation. 'That woman!'

'Excuse me?' Kim was surprised by this.

'My ex-wife. She was jealous of us!'

'Of who?' For a moment, Kim thought he had a lover.

'My daughter and I. We were very close, you know? She adored me and I adored her. Gladys couldn't stand it.'

'Your wife was jealous of her own daughter?'

'Yes, she was. And she took revenge.'

'How?' Kim realised her voice was quite high. 'Sorry. Do you mind telling me?'

'When Tracy was nine, Gladys told me she wasn't my daughter. I knew she'd been flirting with other men, so I didn't doubt it. I left.' He put his head down and covered it with his hands. 'Why did I believe her?'

'How do you know she was lying?'

'Many years after, I spoke to a friend of hers. Gladys had told her that she'd said that to spite me.' He was still crying. 'It wasn't true! Tracy was my daughter!'

'Why didn't you look for her?' Kim wanted to know.

'Time had passed. Tracy was sixteen by then. I wasn't very sure what I was going to tell her, eventually, I went to my wife's house. Tracy had left home. Gladys didn't know where she was and wasn't interested either. She said, "You were so pathetic, you and your little precious princess. You disgusted me how you loved each other!" Then, she laughed and added, "But I won, didn't I? Now you don't have your little princess and she doesn't have you!" I wanted to kill her, right then, right there.' He brushed his hand through his thinning hair as if he wanted to delete those thoughts from his mind.

Kim was in tears. 'How could a mother be so evil?'

'She was evil...' Mr Morley's voice was soft.

'So, you never saw your daughter again?'

'I did. I hired a private investigator and he found her. He told me she met her friends at Dracut Street. It's in a very bad area. Dangerous. Lots of drugs and prostitution. They were there almost every afternoon -outside a big garage door- they were there for hours, smoking, drinking beer... I observed her from a distance many times.' His face revealed he was contrite. 'They were a bad crowd.'

'What do you mean a bad crowd?'

'I don't know...' He shifted on his chair. 'They had lots of bitterness. I suppose Tracy did as well. Every four words they said, three of them were swearing words. The young men had their heads shaved, they had studs and tattoos on their faces. So did the girls.' He went pensive. 'Not my girl... Tracy didn't have anything on her face.'

'Funny.' Kim whispered remembering the reason that brought her to England in the first place. Mr Morley didn't hear. He was absorbed in his own story.

'I took courage one day and I started to speak to her. I was so nervous I couldn't remember what I said. She was smoking. She took the cigarette out of her mouth, blew the smoke into my face and then, flicked the cigarette at me. She turned around and started to walk away. I never tried to speak to her again after that. Although, I did see her from the distance from time to time. Until I lost track of her again.'

'Do you know any of her friends?'

'Yeah. The one who told me Tracy was in Australia. Mrs Jordan. She married a Scott.'

'Where does she live?'

'At Number 36 King Street.'

Kim looked at her grandfather half smiling, half crying.

'Your face...' the old man started to say.

She nodded. 'My name is Kim. I am Tracy's daughter.' Both crying, they both embraced each other.

Kim told her grandfather what their life had been in Australia. She told him about her father but didn't tell him the police suspected her mother. Neither did she tell him what brought her to England.

After three and a half hours of talking, Kim left with tears in her eyes. 'I will visit before going back to Australia.'

'Please, do.'

Back in the luxury of the hotel, Kim was writing in her book.

"Now I know why Mum told me they were both dead."

Looking at the laptop screen, she checked the address her grandfather gave her for Mrs Jordan on Google maps.

When Maud opened her front door she was perplexed to see a tall slim, smart lady on the other side.

'Maud? Maud Jordan?' Kim spoke with a soft voice.

'Yes.' Maud looked at Kim from top to toe. 'Who are you?'

'My name is Kim, I'm Tracy's daughter. I believe you were friends at the end of the eighties when your son and I were very little.'

'Oh my God! Kim! Look at you! You look like Grace Kelly!'

'I hope it's ok to arrive here just like this.'

'Sure it is! I'm so happy to see you!'

'My grand-father gave me your address.'

'Oh. Yes. Mr Morley.' She gestured to Kim to come in. 'What about your mother? Didn't she come with you?'

'She passed away a few months ago.'

'Oh! I'm so very sorry.' Maud patted Kim's arm. 'She was such a good lady. What happened to her?'

'She was sick for a few months… cancer.'

'Oh, God… Poor woman!' There was silence for a moment, 'Well, I'm very happy you came to visit me, Kim.' She paused. 'Would you like to have some tea?'

'That would be lovely. Thank you.'

Then, she started to walk towards the kitchen. Kim spoke loudly. 'How did you meet my grandfather?'

'In church.' She came back to the sitting room. 'Funny. Your mother never mentioned her parents.' She sat down. 'One day we were helping with a few things in the community hall and I had a book. Inside that book, I had a picture of the two of us, as a bookmark and he saw it. '

'And he knew it was his daughter.'

'Yes. He picked it up and looked at it.' Maud's face turned sad. 'He was almost in tears.' She breathed deeply. 'I asked him if he knew my friend and he told me she was his daughter! My! Did I have a shock!'

'So… you started to talk about Mum?'

'Yes. I told him we had gone together with the kids to the park and things like that. Then, I told him you all went to Australia.'

'Yes. He said so.'

'Poor man. He was so sorry he lost contact with her. He didn't tell me much. It pained him to talk about it.' After a moment of silence, she said with a more cheerful voice, 'I'll put the kettle on.'

'Were you a very close friend to Mum?' Kim followed her to the kitchen.

'Yes, I was.' The kettle started to boil. 'We met at a toddler's group. I went there with my Jimmy and she went with you. We became friends.'

'Did you know my father?'

'Not really, but I saw him once.' She looked at Kim. 'He was very handsome.' After a moment she added, 'you take after him in height. Your Mum was much shorter. But you've got her green eyes and blond hair. Your father had dark hair and dark eyes.'

'I know.' She leaned on the edge of the kitchen counter and crossed her arms. 'What else do you know about him?'

'Not much. Your mother was very introverted, you know? She kept to herself.'

'But,... did you have the feeling she was happy?'

'Well, at least happy enough. They had money. They had a beautiful big house in Hampstead Heath.' She gave the tea to Kim. 'They also had a few people employed in the house.'

'Do you know where my father worked?'

Maud was surprised by that question.

'Mum kept to herself even with me. She never told me much. She spoke about the accident, referring to Dad's death...' She looked at the lady to see her reaction.

'Oh, what a business! Who could have done that to your poor father!'

'Indeed.' She left the teaspoon on the sink. 'It distressed Mum to talk about Dad.'

'I imagine.' She sipped her tea. "But I can't tell you where your father worked. I never asked and...' She looked again at Kim, 'your mother never told me.'

'But you are sure my mother was happy.'

'Yes. Sure.' Maud frowned. Then, she became pensive. 'You know... I've got a card somewhere... with a phone number... a lady who could help you more than me.' She was busy looking inside a big drawer.

'Oh, this is the messy drawer. It's like a box of memories... Here it is! When you were two and a half, your nanny left to get married. She said, from that moment, she would only take care of her own children. Anyway, I gave her the phone number of the lady I had.'

'If I was two and a half, it must have been just before we moved to Australia.'

'Yes. It was.'

Kim took the card. 'Did you know any of her friends before she married Dad?'

'No.' Then, again, 'wait!

'Yes?'

'I remember once we were meeting at a park, Jimmy had been crying a lot and made me arrive quite late. When I arrived, she was sitting on a bench, talking to a lady.'

'You know who she was?'

'No. When I arrived to join them, they stopped talking.'

'She didn't even tell you her name?'

'She must have, but I don't remember. She said she was a nurse working at Queen Charlotte's hospital in Chiswick. She had a crystal eye and it was very badly done. I mean, you could see straight away that it was crystal. She must be retired by now. She looked older than us and I'm now 63.' Maud's mind was far away. 'The woman was very happy because she had been made the sister of the ward.'

With little conviction, Kim went to Queen Charlotte's hospital.

'I'm looking for a nurse who was the sister of the ward in 1990. I don't know her name. She's probably retired.' As Kim was talking to the young dark hair receptionist, an old nurse came by.

'Do you know who the sister was in 1990?' the Receptionist asked.

'She had a crystal eye...' Kim said.

'Oh yeah. That was Sister Enid.'

'Great! Do you have her address?' Kim looked at the two of them. They didn't want to give Enid's address to Kim.

'Alright, let's do something.' Kim told them. 'You call her on the phone and I'll speak to her.'

The receptionist and the nurse looked at each other.

'Look, my mother was her friend. We moved to Australia and they haven't seen each other for a long time. Mum passed away and I want to tell her.'

The receptionist looked again at the old nurse. The nurse nodded.

After the receptionist introduced herself, she passed the phone to Kim.

'Sister Enid? My name is Kim. I wanted to talk to you about my mother, Tracy Morley. I believe you know her from the sixties or early seventies, when all of you used to meet at Dracut Street, by a garage door.'

Sister Enid gave Kim her address but said she couldn't meet her for another two days.

After a few days of being in London and moved by her anxiety to know about her mother, Kim hadn't seen much of the British capital. Taking advantage of the two days she had to wait for Sister Enid, she organised to visit some of the sights that the metropolis offered.

As she climbed up the stairs of Westminster's train station reaching the footpath, her eyes went straight to the tower of the Palace of Westminster. She lifted her head up slowly until her eyes finally stopped at the clock of the Big Ben. She was impressed by the height of the tower. She loved Westminster Abbey and despite all her emotions from the last days, she felt good at the Royal Festival Hall in Embankment.

At Waterloo Station she simply observed people coming and going. Most of them were young people with backpacks, probably going to Europe on the Eurostar. "Funny," she though, "A 170-year-old station and I feel like I'm somewhere in the future."

She decided to walk along the river until her feet ached.

She left London Bridge and the tower of London for her second day. Camden Market in Camden Town and Kensington Palace with all the parks around would have to wait for the last days. As well as San Paul's.

∼

Sister Enid lived in a modest flat in Chiswick. She was older than Kim's mother and was dressed neatly and plain. Her long white hair was tied up in a simple low ponytail.

'Thank you for agreeing to meet me.'

'Sure, I'm very eager to know about your mother.'

'Well, I'm sorry to tell you she passed away a few months ago. Cancer.'

'I'm so sorry to hear that. She was a very nice lady. Although...'

'Yes?' Kim was restless to hear what Enid had to say.

'Well,' she looked down and then she looked at Kim. 'They were dark times for all of us. We were all... angry! Annoyed! Rebelling against something or somebody.' She breathed deeply. 'It was when I lost my eye. I was a very disobedient daughter and my father had a short temper. We had lots of arguments. One day, he hit me very strongly with the iron, by the pick. I was nineteen. After I left the hospital, I left home. A couple of years after that, my father passed away and I returned to live with Mum.'

'I'm so sorry.'

'We all have our cross to bear!'

Kim felt bad about changing the subject, but at the same time, she didn't want to dive too deep into Enid's wounds. 'What can you tell me about my mum?'

'I remember Tracy the first time she came. She was so lost. She really hated her mother and she had some feelings of abandonment.'

'Yes. I believe her father left.'

'That's right. Her father was the one who loved her, and he left.' Enid went silent for a moment. 'More than that, I can't tell you. She kept to herself. Certainly, she never opened up to me.'

'What did you do when you met at that place?'

'Well, we did smoke.'

'Cigarettes?'

'Pot.' Kim looked down and Enid looked away. After a while that felt to Kim very long, Enid spoke again. 'Everyone was in their own world. There was no communication, apart from complaining about things and people.'

'What did Mum complain about?'

'As I said, she didn't talk much. I think she was one of the most lost ones.'

'Did she have any special friend?'

'After I left, I heard she hung around with Tommy.'

'Who was Tommy?'

'He was the leader of the group. He wasn't a good person. He would kick anything in his way, like a street bin or street lamp… Once he got a bat and smashed a car's front window.'

'Just like that? With no provocation?'

'Yes. Just like that.'

'And Mum was his girlfriend?'

'No, while I was there, but I bumped into Sarah once and she told me they were together.'

'How could Mum love such a destructive man?'

'She was looking for somebody to love her. I suppose she confused love with sex. It happens more often than it should.'

'She was looking for a father figure?'

'Maybe.'

'Weren't there other men?'

'Darling, everybody there was a mess.' After a moment she added, 'I suppose your mother was flattered that the leader of the group liked her and he probably was happy that a young and beautiful girl like your Mum liked him. Sarah told me she would do anything he asked.' She sighed. 'I doubt there was much actual love between them.'

'That sounds quite disturbing.'

'Indeed. Anyway, when I came back to live with Mum in this flat…' She looked around as if waiting for the flat to confirm her story, 'I got my act together, turned my life around and started to train as a nurse. Obviously, the first thing I did was to leave the group. I only saw your mother some years later. She was sitting on a bench, in the park, waiting for a friend. She had a little girl with her. I suppose it was you.'

'Yes. I am an only child.' Then, Kim asked, 'What did she tell you when you saw her that time?'

'She told me she married well. After living in Ealing for a little while, she and her husband moved to Hampstead Heath. They had a big house there.' She paused for a moment. 'She was going to tell me more, but her friend arrived. I suppose her friend didn't know about her life in Dracut Avenue.'

'So, when you left the group, Mum wasn't with Tommy yet.'

'No. Not even a hint they wanted to be together.'

'Were there any... black people?'

'No. At least not for the two years I was there.'

'Any contact with black people?'

'Not that I saw.' Her mind was miles away. Then with a more assertive voice, she said, 'Sarah was there for a long time. She might be able to answer your questions better than me.'

'Sarah?'

'Yes. Another one of "the lost ones"!'

'Do you know where she lives?'

Sarah was very tall and extremely slim, had pink spiky hair and silver earrings in her nose and ears. Her fingers were also covered with silver rings.

She was wearing a tight black top and black leggings, with a short pink skirt. She was chewing gum and didn't speak when she opened the door.

'Sarah?' Kim was quite intimidated.

'Who's asking?'

'I believe you were a friend of my mother.'

'What?'

'My mother was Tracy Morley.'

'Tracy Morley?'

'Yes. When you all met at Dracut street, by the garage door? In the late sixties...'

'Oh yeah. Well, she hasn't been my friend for a very long time.' She went inside and sat on the sofa. Hesitantly, Kim followed. The flat where Sarah lived was very small, just the room they were in and there were two doors, probably one of them was a bedroom and the other a loo. In a corner, there was a sink and a cooker.

'My mother passed away recently.'

'Sorry.' She moved her hand as if saying, what do you want me to do about it?'

'I don't know anything about her. I grew up in Australia and Mum never told me anything about her life here.'

'Not much to tell.'

'How old were you when you were friends?'

'I think we were fourteen when we met. She disappeared when we were twenty-two.' She looked at Kim. 'What do you want to know?'

'Did you meet at Dracut Street for a long time?'

'Yeah.' She lit a cigarette.

'Did my mum have a boyfriend?'

'She was involved with Tommy. But don't worry. He's not your father.'

'Yeah. I know… I was born when Mum was thirty-four.'

Kim didn't know how to ask what she wanted to know, so she just dived into it. 'Was Tommy a black man?'

'Prffrrf. Sarah was so surprised by the question it made her swallow the smoke and cough. She laughed and then on a more serious note, said, 'we were all white. Pale skin all of us.'

Kim was hesitant.

'Did you have any contact with black people?'

'Look. I've got to go to work. I've got a shift of three hours' Sarah's tone was abrupt. 'So, you'll have to leave.' She stood up and put a coat on her,

'Where do you work?'

'None of your business.'

When they both headed for the front door, Kim stopped and Sarah walked hastily away.

Then Kim decided to follow her.

She saw Sarah entering a hippy clothes shop. Kim went window shopping and then to a cafe until three hours passed. Then, she saw her coming out.

'Have you been following me?'

'I just want some information.'

'About what?' Sarah started to walk, almost running, and Kim was following her.

'About all of you. Who you were, what you did. You laughed before when I asked if Tommy was black. Why?'

'Look, if your Mum didn't tell you anything, maybe it was for a reason.'

'If my mother were alive, I'd ask her. But she's not.'

'So… we all have to die one day.'

'Please!' Kim grabbed Sarah's arm.

'We were high most of the time, ok?' Sarah looked at Kim straight to her eyes. 'And if we weren't high we were drunk.' In a lower voice, she said, 'happy?'

'There was something to do with black people!'

Sarah stopped walking. She leaned on a car.

'Please tell me and I'll leave you alone.'

'Fine! We did horrible things to black people.' Her voice was calm. 'I want to forget about that and I suppose your mother also wanted to forget.'

'Why did you do horrible things to black people?'

'I don't know.' She paused 'I suppose Tommy was the one who made us do things. When he got tired of kicking and breaking things, he took it out on black people and he dragged us all with him.'

'Did my mother do anything?'

'No. She didn't. And that was her problem with Tommy. Tommy was a bastard racist.'

'Was?'

'He's dead now. Hope he's burning in hell.'

'My mother married a black man.'

'Really?' Sarah was really surprised by that fact.

'Yes. She married him when she was forty.'

'Ha!' Sarah tsk-tsked.

'So… she didn't do anything?'

'She did get some tattoos to please Tommy. But that wasn't enough for him. He started to beat her.'

'Oh my God!'

'Do you really think your mother wanted you to know all this?'

'I needed to know it. When she passed away, we removed all her rings from her fingers and we saw the tattoos.'

'She still had her plastic rings?'

'No. They were all gold.'

'Oh! yeah. I heard she married a rich man..'

'Did you meet him?'

'No. She never introduced us.' She sighed. 'Look kiddo. I have to go.' With these last words, she quickly walked away.

Kim stood still in the middle of the footpath.

From the first moment she landed in London, the loving image she had of her mother had been turned upside down and in its place, this terrible figure surrounded by hate and frustration was emerging without any foreseeable end. Kim wasn't sure at this moment what more disasters would be revealed.

She was satisfied she'd found the answer to the question that originally made her come to London, but she now had more questions than she'd started with, and they were more serious. Did Tracy kill her husband? Kim's own father? And if she did it, why?

One thing was clear; her life was in turmoil with nobody to save her.

With the card that Maud had given her, in her hand, Kim arrived at her old nanny's address.

'Hello, are you Penny?'

'Yes.'

'You used to be a nanny for me?'

Penny seemed to be lost.

'My name is Kim. I'm Tracy's daughter. I believe you took care of me in 1990.'

'Oh yes! That's right! How are you? My goodness, you're a grown woman.'

Kim smiled, may I ask you a few things?'

'Sure.'

Penny opened the door to let Kim in.

'What can you tell me about that time?'

'I... I don't know...'

'Did you stop being my nanny because we went to Australia?'

'No.' She looked down. 'I think your mother got upset with me and told me to leave.'

'Why?'

'She left me with you and then your father came home, so I left. I went to the supermarket to buy some food and I saw her there. She went mad! I told her I hadn't left you alone, your father was with you, but she told me not to bother to come back and she left her shopping trolley full of groceries and ran to the car.'

'She got mad because you left me with my dad?'

'Yes. Then I heard what happened to your father.'

'Did the police interview you?'

'No.' She was pensive. 'Now that you mention it... I suppose I should have been interviewed. I was the last person to see your father alive. Apart from you, obviously.'

Kim stared at her.

'You don't think I killed your father!'

'No. No. Of course not!' In a lower voice she added, 'But it is as you say if you were the last person to see my father alive, you should have been interviewed.'

'Well, I had been working there for only two weeks. I don't think anybody knew I was there.'

'Mum did.' Kim's words were hardly audible. Then with a more assertive voice, she asked, 'Do you know the previous nanny?'

'No. But your mother made a comment, when I first applied for the job, that she'd give me a chance before going to the agency she used.'

'You know the name of the agency?'

'Yes. Helga's Nannies.'

After talking to the agency, Kim got the name of her first nanny and headed to the address she was given..

'Yes, how could I forget your mother? She was my last client. Also, all that business with your father's death.'

'Do you know who did it?'

'How could I?'

Kim could see her old nanny was lying. 'Look Mum is dead. Nothing that you say could make matters worse. But I need to know.'

'I don't know why you think I know anything.' The nanny was avoiding Kim's eyes.

'Please.'

'Why do you want to know? Wouldn't it be better to leave things as they are?'

'No!'

'The truth could be hard to handle.'

'I came all the way from Australia to find out. I can see you know quite a lot. You have to tell me!' Kim looked at the nanny. 'Please!'

The nanny looked down and shook her head.

'Look, it is true that I don't know who did it.'

'But you suspect Mum. Don't you?'

She nodded.

'I don't know what happened at that time. But I know what happened at other times.' It was very difficult for her to carry on speaking.

'Please I can't go home not knowing.'

'Your father abused you!'

'What?'

'Your mother caught him twice putting his hand down there. And... the finger inside.'

Kim ran to the loo and threw up.

The old lady followed her. 'You wanted to know.'

Kim washed her face. Then she vomited again. After a few moments, she composed herself. 'So, you think she caught him for the third time and she killed him.'

The nanny didn't answer, just stared at her. After a few moments, she spoke again. 'Your father was a strange person. He really scared me.'

Kim thought about her paternal grandparents.

'He inherited his parents' money. Didn't he?'

'Yes. He did.'

The two ladies went back to the sofa and sat. 'I understand that your mother was alone and saw stability and security with your father.'

'But he wasn't a good person.'

'What do you think? A man who abuses his own child!'

Kim put her head in between her legs. 'I can't remember a single thing about him.' The nanny patted her back. 'I'll make tea.'

Back in her hotel, a sudden feeling of sadness and exhaustion came over Kim. She'd finished her quest. It was all over. Or maybe not? This trip would mark a before and after. A beginning of a new concept of life.

She felt like she had discovered a new world she knew nothing about, and the worst of it was that it was her own world.

She was furious at her mother for having blocked her out of it. Although, she had to admit that confessing that story to a daughter wasn't an easy thing to do. She was also sad for the life her mother had before going to Australia. Tracy had a caring father who loved her so much, and yet, she was all alone in the world.

The emotions were so powerful, Kim started to cry.

Two hours later, her eyes were puffy and still wet and her mood hadn't improved.

She switched off all the lights and went to sleep.

Kim was waiting for Malcolm in a cafe. Next to her table was a young lady with a three-year-old girl. She was blonde with curly hair and green eyes. Kim softly smiled as if she were looking at herself and imagining she was in Ealing Green playing with little Jimmy.

Suddenly she noticed Malcolm, sitting next to her. They looked at each other for a moment in silence.

'I went to London.' Kim started. 'I didn't tell you I was going there to find out what happened because I wasn't very sure I could find anything.'

'I know you were in London.'

'Who told you?'

'Your friend, Lee.'

Kim was surprised he talked to her friend, but didn't want to ask any questions, just remained silent, waiting for her step-father to say something more. But Malcolm didn't open his mouth.

'The first thing I did was to go to the registry office.'

Kim related her adventures in London to Malcolm, step by step. She didn't leave anything out.

Malcolm listened attentively while looking at the kid at the next table, imagining Tracy when she was a little older than that girl and her father left. The narrative was becoming very heavy on Malcolm's shoulders, but he didn't want to stop Kim from talking. By the time Kim finished, he had tears in his eyes.

'I know it must have been very hard for you to see those tattoos on Mum's fingers, but there was a reason and the reason was that she was alone and wanted somebody to love her. Unfortunately, the one she chose was a bastard racist and those tattoos were the way she thought she could get to his heart.'

Malcolm nodded.

'Before returning to Australia, I went to see my grandfather again. He was very happy to see me and I to see him.'

'Did you tell him all your discoveries about his daughter?'

'No. Obviously, not. He didn't know about my father. I told him that he was killed and Mum decided to move to Australia. I also told him that she found happiness by your side.' She paused. 'You'll meet him.'

'Will I?'

'I'm sending money for him to come.'

'Isn't he too old to take such a long trip?'

'He's eighty-five and quite fit.' Kim looked towards the little girl. 'That's probably why things went so wrong. They were too young when they became parents.' With a happier face, she added. 'The two of you will get on very well.'

Malcolm smiled. 'Thank you.'

'What for?'

'For going to London. For telling me.'

Malcolm put his hand over Kim's hands. 'You know… there are some techniques now that can remove tattoos. Why didn't she do it?'

'I don't know. That technique is quite new, by the time it came out, she probably thought the rings were protecting her.'

'Maybe.'

A few days later, Malcolm was by Tracy's grave with a big bunch of flowers. He kneeled and started to cry.

THE END

Leilani's Magick

Irina Gladushchenko

For as long as she could remember, Leilani talked to her flowers.

Every day, she would go out into her garden and talk to her flowers. She would speak about any matter she needed to discuss, to get a different perspective on, to complain about, or to confide in. The plants were attuned to her emotions and knew which part of the garden to guide her towards. When she was in pain, she would always end up where she felt most supported: on the garden bench under the blooming linden tree in summer; under a thick, evergreen canopy on a rainy autumn day; comfortably tucked between the rowan bushes that protected her from the harsh winter elements; or next to the lilacs in spring, breathing in their sweet perfume.

Family, friends, and neighbours very much appreciated Leilani's gift with flowers — the way she was able to care for the flowers and through the flowers — and all of them knew to go to her with their garden (and not so garden-related) questions. She did her best to support them by being open to whatever was within them that was seeking a way to emerge. She always began by anchoring herself and her guests in the most suitable part of the garden. Once she felt the stillness, she encouraged her guests to open up and to trust the healing process.

Leilani was very aware that there was a set of rules to gardening life. And she knew that these rules applied not only to the practical management of a garden, but also to the code of harmonious living. For example, each plant's physical and emotional needs had to be respected for the whole garden to prosper. And there were so many needs and sensitivities to consider! There were the obvious ones including soil and water quality, sunlight position, and exposure to the elements. But there were also more subtle aspects to think about such as colour coordination, grouping, visibility, life cycle, and the most crucial one of them all: vibration! This aspect was not only crucial to the overall health of a garden, but also to the health of all sentient beings. Leilani believed that certain emotions and thought patterns, such as joy, peace, and acceptance, created high-frequency vibrations and an overall harmonious atmosphere. In contrast, other feelings and mindsets, such as frustration, despair, fear, and an inability to listen, vibrated at a lower frequency and caused dissonance. Leilani loved to help others tune in to the unique frequency that enabled them to live to their full potential.

⁓

One afternoon, her cousin Aella came rushing in. She had with her a perfect, green cutting of a Clematis plant. Leilani studied both of them for a moment before inquiring about the issue.

"You see, my dear," Aella explained, "I find it so frustrating that this perfect plant has stopped flowering. It never happened before, but two summers ago it stopped flowering, almost like it decided to have a break. My cottage isn't the same without it! I checked all the essentials, topped up its nutrients, but there has been no change whatsoever."

Leilani listened carefully and then reflected, "Aella, dearest, you say it started two summers ago — did anything change in your life at that time, or a bit earlier than that?"

"Nothing comes to mind other than my grandson's birth at the beginning of that year. We were waiting for the Clematis to blossom, so we could have a family portrait taken in front of our home with three generations, but it never came to flower. So frustrating!"

"Yes, your beautiful, curious little Felix. Did you know that the buttercup plant family is extremely poisonous for young children? Do you think that perhaps the plant was trying to tell you something?"

"Oh, yes, I did know! My mother told me about it when my daughter was a baby! We had to trim the plant so that it was out of reach for little Agnia. Thank you for reminding me!" Aella sighed with relief.

"Thank you for remembering. Would you like a cup of tea?"

Leilani smiled.

Her heart was singing as she marveled at the plant's intelligence. They enjoyed a beautiful afternoon together, strolling through the garden, laughing and sharing memories. While exploring, the cousins found a perfect spot for the Clematis next to the new garden arch. They filled a garden pot with a rich soil and compost mixture, topped it with grit, and planted Aella's beautiful cutting.

Leilani and Aella were transported to their childhood, when they loved playing in their grandmother's magical garden as little girls. Leilani's garden welcomed this lightness.

One night, Leilani had a frightening and vivid dream that made her get up and run outside. In her dream, she turned the TV onto the news channel. The reporter was talking about a new government water preservation initiative, with the aim of centralising all garden areas and to allow home-owners to keep only essential vegetable patches on private properties. All plants of the specified excluded categories would be replanted in a designated closed space with no "visitation" rights by the original owners.

When she awoke to a beautiful sunrise, kneeling, her arms wrapped around a massive lavender bush, she suddenly remembered running with bare feet in the inky darkness, with only a delicate light shining from the full moon hiding behind the clouds. The moonlight highlighted the silvery tips of the lavender bush as if it was showing her the way. The softness of the leaves and the calming aroma of the lavender were just what she needed to process the shock of her nightmare.

Later that morning, while having a cup of tea back in her garden, Leilani was hit with the realisation that the weird dream was a defining moment in her life. She felt like she needed to share this with someone, so she rang Helen, a lady to whom she was introduced at a garden tea party a few years earlier. They had several terrific conversations concerning all things flowers; and Helen had also mentioned that she was into dreams and their significance.

She suggested they have a video call so she could observe Leilani's body language and facial features as she told her story. Leilani agreed and shared her dream in every detail during the call.

"How did you feel when you woke up?" Helen asked.

"Horrified, but very determined at the same time."

"Did you know that it's all about us, even when we dream of other people, things, places?"

"How so?"

"Well, it's like a movie. Our subconscious mind is like a movie director, and it very carefully selects the cast for each role."

"How intriguing! And it does make sense! But what about the garden, the news, and the sense of urgency and importance that I felt with it?" asked Leilani.

"What does a garden represent for you?"

"Peace, beauty, communication, nourishment, memories... life itself, I feel." Leilani gave a deep sigh of contentment.

"And the media?" Helen continued.

"A loud voice," Leilani heard herself replying. "And a sense of urgency, like these are truly BREAKING NEWS stories."

"And what are these breaking news stories about?"

"The fact is that we are killing our planet, our beautiful garden, and there is no time to waste. So we need to always listen to the wisdom Mother Nature offers and follow with our actions. The only legacy that counts is our contribution to this megaproject, Earth," Leilani replied.

"Congratulations on connecting with your vision! And blessings for a beautiful road ahead!"

Leilani thanked Helen for her fantastic support by clarifying her subconscious vision and connecting with her own sense of urgency about healing the planet before it was too late. She knew she needed to do something to create a legacy and an energetic imprint. They ended the call and Leilani immediately went to the kitchen to make a cup of tea. She needed a strong elixir after such a powerful exploration, and more clarity about the practicalities.

One of Leilani's many rituals was her cup selection. Sometimes, it was done blindly, almost like random tarot card picking. This time, there was no hesitation.

"Ahh, the yellow rose!"

Leilani picked out the yellow rose cup and crafted a lovely cup of tea with freshly picked culinary lavender and German chamomile. The ritual and the specific aromas in the yellow rose cup brought back memories of her friend Gerard and how they planted a yellow rose in her garden, late one golden summer's day to celebrate his love for nature and human warmth just a month before his passing. In his goodbye letter to Leilani, he wrote these beautiful words:

Yellow Rose is the purest hope of a summer glow.
Calmed by your mellow tones I carry onto the infinite flow.

She carved those words on a garden sign and added the yellow rose cup to her collection.

As she repeated his soft words in her heart, a thought suddenly came to her. *My energetic imprint, my contribution could be as simple as teaching others about gardening, plant intelligence, and the interconnectedness of everything and everyone!* Leilani felt like her happy self again.

As new neighbours came to check on the lush community garden in Leilani's street, she welcomed them with a big smile and her new book, the "Garden Magick toolkit". One couple shared with her that the key reason they chose this area for their family to move to, was their love of gardening and the "Stories from my Garden" on Leilani's podcast they enjoyed so much.

As members walked through the community garden, their attention was brought to the glowing, clear, yellow flowers in full bloom. "Echinacea 'Leilani'", a garden sign read. The name 'Leilani' suited this elegant plant very well as it had strong upright presence and offered encouragement and healing in a very gentle way.

THE END

The White Shoe

Maria P Frino

Charlie & Margaret
   Sydney
   Present day

The laneway leads me through to a place I don't think I've ever been, but it seems familiar. I try to remember and ask the child who is also alone on this lonely street. Why is the child alone? I ask but he doesn't answer. Looking up the street, it is grand and imposing. It looks even more familiar now. Still, my mind can't place where I am.

There are shoes strewn throughout the street, of all colours and styles – heels, boots, sport shoes, one of every style. I pick up a white shoe and I recognise it immediately; it is my first wife's shoe from our wedding. Why is my wife's shoe here in front of me when she died years ago? The street, the lonely child, the shoes… and the only thing I remember is this white heeled court shoe.

I try remembering my first wife but right now I can't even remember her name. How do you forget someone you loved and lived with for years? What I do know is she died of breast cancer. I keep gazing down this amazing street trying to place it.

Oh, now I know. This is the street where she was born and is that our child? I don't remember us having children.

My feet drag as I walk into my home. The day has not yet begun, dawn is peeping through the darkness. The house is quiet, Margaret isn't up yet, and Jasper raises his eyes looking at me without moving. I give him a pat, "No need to move mate, it's early."

Pulling my shoes off I drop them in the kitchen corner. I've brought the white shoe home with me, although I'm not sure why. I decide to leave it with my other shoes in the laundry cupboard. Exhaustion has taken over; it was a long walk to that street.

Switching on the kettle, I brush my fingers through my thinning hair then reach up to find my favourite mug. A soothing tea will wake me up.

"You're up early."

Margaret has come into the kitchen and begins making a tea for herself. "I know, but I woke up and decided not to try to fall back to sleep again. What are your plans for today?" I avoid letting her know I slept walked again.

"The university has asked me to come in and go over the research papers. I'll be there all day. Come and join me for lunch if you like."

"Oh, thanks. It will be nice to venture out on what should be a pleasant Spring day."

"Great, I'll see you at one. Usual place." She takes her steaming mug with her to the bedroom to prepare to go to work on her day off.

Me? Well, I'm retired so I have a full day to fill with whatever I want to do.

∼

"Charlie, how nice to see you." I'm sitting with Margaret at our favourite café when her colleague greets me.

"James, good to see you too," I answer and shake his hand. I have a suspicion he has a thing for Margaret but I've never been able to confirm it. He seems to have a look in his eye when he greets her and it's more than just professional awe. Like how he's looking at her now.

"Margaret, I'll see you after lunch. Enjoy it, both of you."

"Cheers, James." I smile watching him walk out of the café. "He seems pleased, have you made progress this morning?" She doesn't notice the sarcasm in my voice.

"Quite a lot, yes. The research is showing that the brain may be mimicking a *'fight or flight'* response."

I don't answer as I take a mouthful of food and wonder whether this is the case for me. I am part of the research study being undertaken by Margaret's department at Sydney University. After this morning's episode I am flustered and decide to change the subject to more mundane topics. We chat as we eat talking generally about us, our dog and our life. When we finish our lunch and I walk her to the university before I head home.

As I open the front door, Jasper looks up at me with wanting eyes. Picking up the lead, Jasper's tail wags even more as he waddles towards me. At fourteen, he's slowed down but still loves his walks. "Come on boy, let's head down to the bay." As we walk, I think about this morning. I won't tell Margaret about this episode yet, not until I've worked out why I remember it. The white shoe has something to do with this, it's a memory from my subconscious.

Down at the bay I let Jasper off-leash and watch him play with the other local dogs. I chat with the dog owners as we bask in the sunshine that bounces off the shimmering water. The boat ramp is damp from last night's rain and a few boats bob about near it. This is my daily routine, a mid-afternoon walk with Jasper. Fourteen years of meeting up with his friends and mine. I'm half-listening as others chat about their week but my mind is on the white shoe.

Jasper and I arrive back home; the sun having warmed us, and Jasper is ready for a nap. He plods off to his mat as I head into the laundry and take out the white shoe. It smells of her, but how is this possible? She's been dead for ten years. I'm also struggling to remember the child because we don't have any children. Who was he and what does he have to do with me?

Hours later Margaret arrives home and finds me sleeping on the lounge clutching the shoe. I see her curious face and point to it. "This? I found it this morning."

"What? Where?"

"Umm, I was on a street. It was familiar but I couldn't place where I was."

"You had another episode?"

"Yes, and I remember it because of this shoe."

She turns away heading to our bedroom, "Right, tomorrow you're coming with me to the university. We have to get to the bottom of your sleep walking."

Charles & Patricia
New York
1950

Charles stretches in his black leather executive chair. Wall Street ushers itself into view as he walks towards the window. His town. His domain. New York is in his blood.

With seven years under his belt as CEO of CZL Financial Services, his clientele includes: oil tycoons, pharmaceutical companies, fashion and movie moguls. His success is attributed to knowing the social elites of New York. This now includes his Fiancée's family, the Rothburghs.

Patricia and he come from old money. She is the socialite keeping his company rich with the right clients. In two weeks they will be married. He feels elated as he thinks of Patricia as his wife. She has planned the event of the year, everyone who is anyone in New York society has been invited. The skyscrapers lick the moody sky, rain is on its way. Still, his mood is fine because he is marrying the girl of his dreams.

He arrives home after work. They have been married for less than a month and he relishes coming home to Patricia.

"Charles, I have some amazing news."

He walks towards her placing his briefcase on the kitchen table. "Good evening my love," he says taking her in his arms kissing her cheek.

"I think you had better sit down. This is sudden I know... I'm pregnant."

Charles remains still, her words floating around in his mind. "What! We only returned from our honeymoon last week." He rubs his hand through his thick curls, "Oh, my love, what wonderful news."

"You scared me for a minute, I thought you weren't pleased when you hesitated."

He kisses her passionately then with his arms outstretched, he takes in her beauty. "How could you think that? This is fantastic, we're going to be parents. When did you find out?"

She proceeds to tell him their doctor had confirmed this afternoon. "It was a honeymoon conception; the baby is due next winter."

He pulls her close again and tightens his hug around her. He is overwhelmed with love because he is going to be a father and couldn't be happier.

Jonathan was born in December. He was a healthy nineteen pounds but is a colicky baby keeping them awake. Three months of little or no sleep is taking its toll on both of them.

Charles was a sleepwalker as a child and since Jonathan's birth, it has returned. Patricia wants him to seek help because he has placed himself in dangerous situations more than once. She found him disorientated and dazed in the middle of Central Park one night. Since that night she has urged him to go and see someone. He eventually listened to her and has been seeing a psychologist for some years now.

"Come on, go and freshen up. I've prepared something special tonight. We have to celebrate our good news."

His body shivers, the cold seeping through him. How can he be cold when he's in bed? Suddenly a man taps his shoulder. What is this man doing in their home? Panic takes over and he punches the intruder who falls flat on the road. Road? What is going on?

He hears her voice. She is screaming his name. It sounds miles away, somewhere in the distance. Now her voice is low, he hears it in slow motion. She is headed towards him and pushes him to the side of the road with urgency. Tyres screech.

A short time later, the police are asking him questions, but his mind cannot comprehend what has happened. His wife and son are lying on the road covered by sheets. They have been run over. And it's all his fault.

"Mr Zellonica, I'm afraid we're going to have to take you to the station. We have more questions to ask."

Charles nods his head and pulls the blanket the police gave him tighter around his shoulders.

Soon after, he has a steaming cup of coffee in front of him and he is sitting in a police interrogation room. Two police officers are asking him questions. He answers as best he can but cannot explain how his wife and son were on the road. In fact, he couldn't answer why he was on the road at four in the morning on this bleak, wintry night.

"The doorman has decided not to press charges, he feels you are suffering enough. He told us he knew you were not in the right frame of mind."

"Doorman? You mean the intruder. He was in our home. I was protecting my family."

"I'm afraid you're incorrect. You were found in your pyjamas on Park Avenue, disoriented and confused. When your doorman tried to help you, you hit him to the ground."

Charles looks at the policeman, the stockier of the two sitting in front of him. "What? I must have been sleep walking. But I'm in therapy and it hasn't happened for a year. This is why Patricia came after me, she was trying to protect me. Then Jonathan must have followed her. Sometimes he wakes up during the night too." Distraught, Charles stops talking knowing he has caused the death of Patricia and Jonathan. Their son was only three.

∽

Sydney

I'm in the university cafeteria. These places are always so nondescript with the plastic chairs and long trestle tables. Margaret is meeting me here when she finishes her notes on the discussions this morning. She had asked me to come to work with her this morning because she wanted me to talk to her research team about the sleep walking episode I had last week. I told them as much as I could remember and I still wasn't able to explain where I was when

I saw the lonely child and the shoes. All I could tell them was that I felt I was in a grand street that is well known.

As I sip the crap coffee, I think about some of the terms I heard this morning. Margaret and her team threw around words and conditions I had never heard of. Words like – parasomnia, somnambulism, non-REM (NREM), RBD and night terrors. We've all heard of dreams, but what the hell are night terrors?

"Sorry Charlie, I was intercepted by someone on my way here." She bends to kiss me as she arrives.

"It's fine. I've been going through things in my mind. I hope I was of some help."

"You were. Those brain tests we did might show some interesting results and that will certainly help us. Now, do you want to eat here? The food is average."

"No, I might head home. I'm exhausted after all this and not that hungry."

"Of course. Well, I'll see you tonight." She bends down and kisses me again.

I watch as my intelligent wife heads back towards her office. She has made this her life's work, to find out why I sleepwalk. Initially, she was researching sleep disorders in general, but since meeting me, she is now specialising her research into finding a cure. Margaret is worried I might hurt myself during an episode and is paranoid she won't wake up in time to help me.

Returning home, I decide to rest. Heading to the lounge I place my mobile on silent and set an alarm for an hour. Sleep comes easily…

"Mummy, wait for me."

The street again, this grand parade. The child is running after his mother…

I wake with a start. It was the child I saw last time. Only this time I saw him fleetingly as he ran towards his mother. She was on the grand street too. I don't remember anything else, but I have this dread that something awful happened. There was something in the child's voice. It was chilling.

Sitting up I brush my face vigorously with my hands as I try to delete this from my mind. I don't know who this child is and it's driving me crazy that I keep thinking of him.

"Jasper," I call, "time for a walk."

As we head to our usual spot near the boat ramp, I wonder whether I should tell someone other than Margaret about what happened. Will they believe me? People know about sleep walking, but do they know that some people can remember things? Will they think I have a mental illness?

By the time I reach the others, I decide to keep things to myself. Margaret will find a cure or at the very least, something to help me. She understands I'm not crazy so there is no need for me to confide in anyone else for now.

∼

I pick up the phone, "Margaret Hughes-Zellonica speaking."

"Mrs Hughes-Zellonica, my name is Anthony Demurie of the Australian Standard. I'm the Health Editor and am interested in interviewing you about your current research project."

"Hello, Anthony. Well thank you, but the research is ongoing, and results are sketchy at best. I don't think I am ready to release anything yet."

"I understand. I would still be interested in interviewing you about your work in general. You have built quite a reputation in the sleep disorders area. Maybe I could include the work of some of your team as well?"

I think about his request and decide to discuss it with my team and the marketing department. "Leave it with me. I'll come back to you after I consult the others."

"Thank you, much appreciated. And thanks for your time now."

Replacing the receiver, I type up an email and send it to my team. I will wait for their response before sending one to marketing.

∼

Later that evening, we're sitting on the lounge watching the nightly news. I'm telling Charlie about the journalist.

"Why not do it? It will be publicity for the university as well as be good for you."

"I wasn't keen at first because he wanted to discuss our current research. You know that it's not at a stage yet where there is something conclusive, but then he still wanted to discuss my work in general."

"Then there is no reason not to do the interview."

"Well, the marketing department has given me the go ahead… and my team, so, yes I'm doing it."

Anthony Demuri, the journalist, is sitting opposite me at my favourite local café. It's a mild Monday with the winter chill not quite a force yet. He has asked me all the questions he wanted to, and I have answered as best I can given I'm not able to speak about the research yet. He is an interesting young man, probably twenty-eight years old. Or he could be thirty-something. Anyway, he has lived in London, did his master's in journalism and then worked for a couple of newspapers while living there. With this experience under his belt, he came home two years ago. He sees this job as a stepping stone to a career in television. He's handsome enough to host a TV show or report the news, his blonde curls and large brown eyes make him pleasant to look at. He is telling me he will send me a draft of the interview to approve before publication, which will be in two weeks. I nod my acceptance surprised I am able to see it before it goes to press.

"Well, thank you for your time. If I have further questions, is it ok if I call you?"

"That's fine, Anthony. Afternoons are the best time to catch me."

After shaking my hand, he walks away. I'm nervous about what light he is going to portray my work in. Most of my work is experimental, which is why I'm not able to discuss a lot of it and for many lay people, the terms and outcomes are quite complicated.

Still, he made me feel comfortable while we were talking so I'm sure he'll be kind to this old science researcher.

∽

Sitting on the bed, I'm waiting to be prepped for yet another test. Margaret has organised more experimental tests and is using me as a guinea pig. Am I nervous about this one? I sure am. They are going to add probes to my head and electrical signals will be sent through my brain from the probes. The side effects may be nausea, blurred vision and feeling generally unwell for a day or two. Still, I know how important it is to Margaret to find a cure for people like me, so I'm here to help her. For me personally, I would be happy never to sleepwalk again because even though I haven't hurt myself or anyone else yet, the possibility is always there.

"Hi Charlie." Margaret's research assistant has walked in. "I'm going to prep you for this test. How are you feeling today?"

"Fine. A little nervous, but otherwise ok."

She smiles but remains silent as she unravels the cords connected to the probes. Asking me to lie down and remain still she begins placing the probes on my forehead, behind my ears and the top of my head. Testing them, she asks me to tell her when the sensation becomes too strong. Within minutes I complain, and she sets the probes to a sensation slightly below what I felt.

"This should be strong enough for us to get some good results. Now, please lie as still as you can, this will only take fifteen minutes."

I turn my eyes towards her and nod slightly. With this she leaves me alone in the room. My thoughts go to the child. A shiver runs through my body, something about him seems so familiar, but I don't know who the child is? Does he have something to do with the white shoe? I decide I will do some research when I arrive home after this test. Although what it is I'm actually looking for, I'm not sure yet.

∽

My computer blinks as it starts up. First, I type in sleepwalking, but most of the links that blink on the screen I have already seen. Then, I type, 'remembering you have been sleepwalking' and again, these are links I have already read. I have to think of this is a different way. Why am I seeing this child? Is the dream trying to tell me something? I spend a few hours researching dream states and what the term 'disassociated arousal' means. Apparently, some sleepwalkers are in a state of half-sleep and sensitivity, and it is these people who remember what they are doing. I'm one of those people and this explains why I'm remembering.

Is it a dream? What is it that makes me sleepwalk? Will I hurt myself or someone else? This last question sends shivers down my spine. I keep scrolling through links and find something called 'RBD'; it is a sleep behaviour disorder. As I keep reading, I discover it is also known as 'parasomnia', which is the undesired things that happen when you are sleeping. This happens when a sleepwalker acts out vivid dreams that are full of action. I had heard Margaret and her team mention these terms during my first round of tests. It is the acting-out action that worries me because it's only a matter of time before something awful happens to me, or worse still, Margaret.

I'm still at the computer when Margaret arrives home. She bends down and greets me with a kiss.

Looking at the screen she says, "Doing some research are you?"

"Yes, after I was at the university last, I came home and had a rest. I dreamt of the child again, he was calling out and chasing after his mother. I have this dread that something awful happened. Do you want me to print out what I've been reading?"

"Sure, any research is valuable."

∼

Sitting in my office my email pings with five messages. They are mostly research papers from my staff, more for me to read later. The one I'm most interested in though is from Anthony, the journalist. Opening it, I quickly scan what he has written, which makes me feel humble and proud. He has painted me in a scholarly light and speaks of my achievements along with those of my team. Closing the document, I save it to my desktop and send a copy to Charlie's email, I'd like to hear his thoughts on this too. I will discuss the article with him tonight.

As I shuffle through the papers on my desk, my eyes rest on Charlie's photo. We met ten years ago; he was still reeling after the sudden death of his wife. We were both at a mutual friend's party and I found out later he had to be dragged along because he still wasn't in the mood to socialise. His wife had been dead for two years at the time. Charlie is a sensitive soul and takes his time to recover when negative emotions rock him.

We connected through our love of musicals and classical music. He has a knack of knowing obscure facts about the actors, the story or the music behind musicals. This makes him a whizz at trivia when these subjects come up. I was amused by his geekiness, and we talked the whole night. What surprised me was that he said goodnight without asking for my number. I thought we had something going, but Charlie is not one for rushing into things.

In the end I asked our friend for his number and called him. We dated for a few months and then he surprised me with a ring. Now this was out of character, but I jumped on the chance before he changed his mind. When I asked him what made him decide so quickly, he shrugged saying, "You're beautiful and I want you in my life. It was an easy decision." We were married at a small ceremony six months to the day we met. Everyone who knows Charlie was surprised at how quickly he made this decision, but I knew the truth and that was all that mattered.

My mind wanders to his dreaming about this child, and I look for the research he has done. Finding it in my emails, I print it out and set it aside with the other papers from my staff. At our next meeting we will go through all this data and information. I breathe deeply, sometimes I wonder whether we will ever find what we're looking for.

∼

Arriving home, Jasper plods over to greet me. "Hey boy, how are you?" I say as I rub his head.

"Hi. How was your day." Charlie is at the oven taking out a roast that will be ready soon. He bastes it and returns it to the oven.

"Good actually. Did you look at the article?"

"I did. You made a great impression on that young journalist."

"He has certainly painted me in a positive light. I can't take all the credit, without my staff, I couldn't do what I do so effectively. Not to mention your research." She smiles and nudges my shoulder.

"Gee, thanks. I'm sure your team helps, and he does give them some of the credit, but ultimately you make the final decisions. This is all you and he recognises this. It's brilliant and I'm proud of you."

He walks towards me and pulls me to him. Kissing me gently, he moves to my ear and whispers, 'I love you'.

I repeat the same words to him realising we don't tell each other this often enough. I make a mental note to say it more often.

"Are you ok with discussing the article further over dinner? I want to know whether it needs changing. I have a couple of things in mind that need revising," I say as he is still holding me close.

"Sure. Why don't you go and freshen up? Dinner will be ready in a few minutes."

I give him a peck on the cheek and head to our bedroom to change. When I come back to the kitchen, the dining table is set with the lamb roast he has prepared.

"This smells great. Now I really am hungry." I look down at Jasper, "You're going to enjoy this bone tomorrow." He looks at me with his tail wagging anticipating he might be having a treat now. "Tomorrow Jasper, now go to your mat." He obediently pads over to his mat, circles a few times, then lies down.

Charlie is already eating as I make my plate. He has a healthy appetite with his plate piled high. He starts the conversation when he finishes his mouthful.

"I didn't find anything needing to be changed, the article reads very well to me."

"Well, that's good to hear, but I need to make a few of his points more succinct. Especially where he talks about some of my previous research, he has skipped some of the things I told him. I think he needs to expand on these points."

"Oh right. I suppose I see what you mean but be careful not to make it too full of science-based terms. Remember, this is a newspaper article, not a piece for your esteemed colleagues."

"Good point, I'll keep that in mind when I'm editing it."

I change the subject to the child and the research Charlie has done. He tells me that knowing more about why he is sleepwalking is comforting, but he is uneasy about what happened to the child.

"Keep in mind this is a dream, don't become anxious about it or it may make your sleepwalking worse."

"I know, I'm trying not to think about it. I wish I was able to control it better."

Telling him this is not possible, I take his hand in mine and pat it reassuringly. This research I'm doing is the only way to fix the problem, and I am determined to find something to help Charlie.

The article is published and the reaction from my staff and colleagues is one of pride. I receive messages from friends who know of my work but didn't know how involved it was with medical breakthroughs. Many of them were pleased to see that part of our research into sleep disorders had led to advances in how to manage sleep apnoea. The smile on my face grows with each message I read. This is all great, but what I really want is to find a cure, or at least something to help manage the condition for people who sleepwalk.

Turning on my computer, I find an email from the Australian Office of Medicine and Medical Sciences. Gasping, I read that I am nominated for a Fellowship Award – For research and development of procedures to prevent disease. As I read the criteria needed to receive this award, I begin to wonder who would have nominated me for this award. I am still reading when the head of my department walks into my office.

"Hi, have you seen the email yet?"

"Yes, I'm reading it now. Wow, I'm blown away."

"It's a great honour, and with only three other women being

awarded prior to this year, it's rare for a female professor to win. We nominated you, the dean and the rest of the faculty thought it long overdue for you to be recognised."

I started my career as a researcher and have now been a professor for twenty-five years. This is a job I love and don't expect to receive anything in return. This, however, is amazing and I tell James how I'm feeling. "Thank you, this is a little overwhelming. It's very generous of you and the others, although something tells me it was you who instigated this."

"I did, but it doesn't matter. The important thing is you're nominated. The ceremony is in a few weeks. I have booked us a table for ten. So, come on Margaret, it's your time to shine," he says as he walks out. "You'll be receiving your invitation soon."

His voice fades away as he walks down the corridor. I pick up the phone and call Charlie to tell him the news. "Yes, isn't it wonderful?"

He is as excited as I am. We talk about how we both feel and he says we will celebrate tonight. He will surprise me. Hanging up the phone, I smile at what a thoughtful husband he can be.

When I arrive home, Charlie has organised a few of our friends to come over and celebrate with us. I walk into kisses and hugs from everyone, with Ursula, my friend I have known forever, hugging me with all of her ninety kilos of loveliness.

"Here you go," says Charlie handing me a champagne flute with bubbles popping, "I know you will be a great Fellow."

There are laughs all round as we all chink our flutes together and talk about the meaning of this award. To have recognition from an esteemed official organisation such as this has me feeling fortunate. To be doing something I am passionate about that is also significant and recognised is amazing. The research my team and I are doing is making inroads into sleep disorders and their management.

We're all sitting at the dining table having finished dinner. Charlie pours more wine. We have all indulged, we're all drunk. My elated feelings are heightened by the alcohol, the stimulating conversation and discussing what Charlie and I will wear to the ceremony.

"I'll do your hair and makeup," offers Ursula. "No offence darling, but you are hopeless when it comes to this."

"Thanks, Ursula. I'd love you to make me look worthy of this honour." Working in a university office, there is no reason for me to wear makeup. And pulling my hair back in a headband is about as much as I do to my hair.

"Well, for this event, I will make you the princess you are meant to be."

I laugh and raise my glass towards her. The conversation continues along this vein of frivolity with more laughs and bad jokes until late in the evening. It's been a long time since Charlie and I entertained and I relish being with this lot, they are our friends who we love dearly. We will always have their support.

The laneway is leading me to the grand street again. This time I see a man, he is disoriented and miserable. Police officers are placing a blanket over his shoulders and leading him to the paddy wagon…

I wake up and am in my lounge room. My eyes adjust to the dimness as I try to make sense of what I saw. Who was that man? I had felt his presence and he looked a lot like my father who died twenty years ago.

Walking into the kitchen, I flick the light switch and see it's three in the morning on the blinking oven clock. I'm thirsty and gulp down a glass of water in one go. Sitting on a dining chair, I am exhausted. How long was I sleepwalking? It felt like a long time, but I only remember a small amount. Frustrated, I head back to our bedroom, I need to have some decent sleep. After our celebration with friends for Margaret's nomination, I haven't slept well. The excitement about the award was probably the reason.

"Good morning." Margaret is making herself coffee, "want some?"

"Yes, double shot please. I'm exhausted." I proceed to tell her about the last two nights' interrupted sleep and the sleepwalking episode.

"The excitement surrounding the award has kept me in a light sleep too. So, any idea who the man is?"

I tell her I have no idea but am curious as to why he looks like my father. "He was instantly familiar to me."

"It's not unusual to dream about your parents, especially when they have passed. I hope this isn't confusing you. Do you think it has anything to do with the child?"

"Possibly. Maybe the child is me and I'm watching my father being taken away. But he was never in prison."

"It could be your subconscious reacting to his death. You are missing him and didn't want him taken away from you."

We both sip our coffee and remain quiet for a few minutes.

"Well, I'm going to play golf today and that will take my mind off all this. I'll be out all day."

"That's great. The fresh air and camaraderie are exactly what you need. Enjoy it, and don't worry about dinner, I'll organise something."

∽

My golf game is affected by my lack of sleep. The frustration shows as I slam my clubs into my golf bag.

"Easy Charlie," says Felix, my friend who won the day.

"It's fine for you, you won. My game sucked today."

"We all have bad days. Come on, let's head for the nineteenth hole, that will make you feel better."

The four of us sit and talk about the game, which makes me even more weary. After an hour I say, "Guys, I'm off, I look forward to a better game next week."

"Good night Charlie," they all say in unison.

I arrive home to the smells of a casserole, one of my favourite meals that Margaret cooks.

∽

I'm in my office trying to concentrate. Last night was the presentation of the Fellow award. The celebration was in the city at one of the plush hotels and Charlie and I were chauffeured to the event. I felt so privileged and when I walked into the ballroom where many of my colleagues were standing, I felt giddy with pride. We had a wonderful night but now my head is telling me otherwise. I reach for two painkillers, wash them down with the last of my water and settle in for the day.

After the article came out, there has been interest from the wider community about the sleep studies and research my department is doing. There are several emails I need to answer as well as more journalists to call. They are chasing me for interviews and I'm wondering how I'm going to fit these into my schedule. Still, I have to manage it because the dean and the board are expecting me to do them.

This sudden interest in our research is somewhat bewildering, I have been researching for twenty years and no one had even asked what I do until now. Now, it seems everyone wants to talk to me. Charlie has quipped that I am a rockstar of the scientific world and that I should lap up all this attention. What would make me happier is if I had something concrete to tell them – that I have found a cure for sleepwalking. And especially for those who remember, because it is these people who are more likely to injure themselves or someone else.

Charlie's episodes have increased in the past few months, and he is intrigued by this man he keeps seeing. The resemblance to his own father is uncanny. The other thing he has realised is that the street this man was standing in is Park Avenue in New York. Was he really sleepwalking all the way to New York? Any wonder he is tired when he wakes up. I shake my head and laugh because my scientific brain is wired to not believe anything that isn't plausible. *Of course, he's not walking all the way to New York!*

Charlie and I have been discussing each episode and as he remembers more, he is diarising what he sees. This is helping him make sense of the story. He thinks the man standing on Park Avenue is someone he knows, but how Charlie is connected to this man, we are yet to work out. I have told him to keep diarising as he remembers and once he has written what he needs to, he is to close the diary and not think about it for the rest of the day or week. I've noticed if he focuses too much on this, he becomes depressed. This is the last thing I want for him.

I finish up with answering all the emails and ready myself for a meeting with my team. They will be waiting for me in the boardroom, and this is where I'm headed.

We have been discussing our latest works in progress for two hours when James walks in. "Hello everyone, sorry to interrupt. Margaret, may I speak with you," he says as he walks out again.

I stand and head out to the hallway where I find him standing against the wall.

"You are on a roll with awards."

I tilt my head, "What are you talking about?"

"You and your team have been nominated for the Flauncey Medal. I received the email and came to tell you after reading it. Congratulations."

"Uh, thank you." Words stay stubbornly in my mouth. I didn't know what to say. This is so soon after the Fellowship award.

"There is more information in the email, you have been sent a copy as well. Now, off you go back in and tell your team. This is another well-deserved accolade." With this he holds my shoulders and kisses both my cheeks.

I feel a red-hot blush rising from my neck and devouring my face. James has never been so friendly with me at work, he is the ultimate professional. I nod more to cover my embarrassment than to acknowledge he is leaving. Charlie has mentioned he thinks James wants me for more than my work, but I brushed him off. Now that James has kissed me, I'm wondering if he does.

This medal is indeed an accolade. It is given only every four years and the competition is fierce. It's a team medal given to a research project for the development of a successful application to prevent and/or manage a chronic illness.

As I walk back into the boardroom, I'm quite stunned we have been nominated because we are still working to find a cure. We do know how to manage chronic sleepwalking, but we are yet to find out why some people remember and why it happens at all. I feel this nomination is a little premature. Sitting down, I discuss what I've been told with my team.

Two hours later I'm back in my office reading the email from the Flauncey Association. Why James had to interrupt our meeting to tell me is puzzling. This is only a preliminary nomination, we are one of twenty departments and universities nominated. From these, three will be picked as finalists. James could have waited until I had read the email, his reaction was premature as well. No one will find out about who the finalists are until November this year, that's nine months away.

Rather than be angry with him, a smile crosses my face. As a department head, James is always keen to spread the word about any accolades the university receives. It means more funding for research projects and the prestige, especially from an accolade as this one, is priceless. I try not to think about the fact he may have a thing for me, and this is the reason he interrupted the meeting.

With the notes I made at the meeting, I begin to transcribe them into my files before I tackle the folders my team handed to me. My job is all consuming and I enjoy the challenges it brings, but sometimes I would like the help of an assistant who works only for me. The three assistants we have on staff are shared between three of the eight departments in this faculty.

We're sitting in the lounge room with the television on. Neither of us is watching it because we've been discussing yet another episode I have had. This time two names came into my head - CZL Financial Services and the Rothburgh family. I have no idea what CZL is or does, but the Rothburgh family is a well-known, old-money family from New York.

"Maybe the Rothburghs have something to do with this CZL company?" says Margaret.

"Possibly. I'll do some research tomorrow, I'm sure there will be something about CZL Financial Services online."

"Well, this is progress Charlie. Maybe you'll find that the Rothburghs have a stake in this company?"

"Probably do. I'll diarise everything I find tomorrow."

Then Margaret proceeds to tell me the news of the nomination. I'm impressed although I agree with her it is too soon to be excited. James does become excited about these awards, not that I blame him. Universities earn many rewards from them, especially the prestigious ones like the Flauncey Medal.

"That's good news and you should be proud of your team. Still, there is time before we break out the champagne. Now, what would you like to watch?"

We settle on a movie, a light romantic comedy that helps to take my mind off sleepwalking for a short time.

The next morning, Margaret leaves for work and after tidying the kitchen, I settle in to do some research. My computer whirrs as I search for my glasses. When I find them, I give Jasper a tickle under his chin and he plods over to his mat. I open the search engine and type in the company name.

The first link that appears is of Charles Zellonica, CEO. "What the…?" I say this out loud and Jasper responds by lifting his head off his mat. "It's ok mate, nothing to do with you," I reassure him. I spend the next two hours going through every link I can find about this man - How he started the company, who his clients were, how he was one of New York's richest men, and then I find why the Rothburgh name had come to me – his wife Patricia was a Rothburgh, the daughter of the youngest brother.

Another two hours passes as I am fascinated to find out more about both Charles and Patricia. Bookmarking all of the links I want to keep, I then open up another tab and type – Peter Zellonica, my father's name. I knew little of his past because he didn't speak of it. My mother was no help because he hadn't spoken to her of it either. All she knew was that there were distant relatives in America that he never mentioned. She found out from my grandmother who had warned her not to bring the subject up with Peter.

Jasper places his head on my knee reminding me it's time for a walk. I was so preoccupied with my research that I hadn't even had lunch. Grabbing an apple and his leash, I say, "Ok, come on. It's time I took a break anyway."

We head out into the sunshine, the autumn day is cool, but the sun warms me as we walk. My head is full of all the information I have found as we walk towards the bay.

∼

New York
Charles and Peter
1939

They are both holding onto the bannister watching the adults below. Their sprawling home is always full of visitors and this Saturday night is no different. The garden party started at three and has moved indoors for the grand dinner. Peter and Charles have had their dinner, but they are curious to see what their parents and their friends are doing.

Charles is fascinated by the men's suits and what the women are wearing. He loves fashion and money. In fact, he is obsessed with both. He is six years Peter's senior and Peter is yet to find his passion. They have enough money, as do most of their friends, so he's not enamoured with it like his brother, Charles. When Peter says *enough money*, he means a lot. They are one of the richest families who live on Park Avenue, along with the Rothburghs.

"Wow, she's a looker," whistles Charles in a whisper. He is watching Patricia Rothburgh as she walks in with her parents. "I should be down there to greet her."

"You would have been had you not spoken so rudely to our parents."

"It was our father's fault, he should not have blamed me for the broken branches on the cherry trees. I wasn't the one riding the horse yesterday, it was the apple of his eye, Beatrice."

He was talking of our little sister who we call Betty when we're not angry with her. She is our father's favourite, and he makes no secret of this. The brothers will never come close to being in their father's favour like Betty. This is something that peeves Charles to no end.

"Still, you cussed, and I understand why father grounded you. This should teach you a lesson, that temper of yours will always land you in trouble."

"Oh, shut up you little twat. Why are you still here anyway? Isn't it past your bedtime? Go on, go. Stop bothering me while I watch the love of my life."

They were not best buddies. They fight constantly, more because Charles doesn't want Peter around. Charles is the better looking one – taller, fitter and more eloquent – he is a ladies' man and doesn't want his little brother ruining his chances. He was also smarter; his brain could figure out equations quicker than anyone. *Me, I'm an average student.* Peter has to concentrate hard to receive the grades Charles had obtained.

They have never been close and Charles' attitude towards him became worse as years passed. He was embarrassed having a brother who didn't meet his standards. Also, he was closer to Betty, but only because she made an effort.

A week after the garden party, the three siblings are dressed in their Sunday best to attend their parents' funeral. Their father was a pilot with his own aeroplane. He and their mother were visiting friends in Texas when an engine blew on the return flight. The four people on that plane died instantly.

Charles was old enough to take care of Betty and Peter, but he wasn't ready for this responsibility. So, the powers that be organised for the children to be cared for by a distant uncle. He was in his sixties, a brash and unforgiving man who only had eyes for Charles.

Peter disliked him instantly and their uncle knew it. Having already decided that he would leave as soon as he was eighteen, it happened sooner because Charles did something that made him leave earlier than anticipated.

After their parents were buried, there was a reading of the will. When Charles heard he was to share his inheritance with both Betty and Peter, he was not pleased. After this he did everything to show Peter up with their uncle. Charles also made Peter the butt of any trouble he caused. Peter was always blamed for things Charles had done. This went on for two years before Peter couldn't take the abuse any longer. At sixteen he left the only home he had ever known with what little savings he had and moved to Los Angeles. From there he travelled to Australia settling in Sydney and never spoke of his family again.

∼

Sydney
    Present Day

After months of researching the Zellonica and Rothburgh families, I had found out that Charles Zellonica was my father's brother and he had married Patricia Rothburgh. She and their son had died the night he had been found in his pyjamas on Park Avenue. This correlates with the dream I have been sleepwalking to.

For some reason, I feel some responsibility for this tragedy. Now I know I'm not, but some part of me feels the weight of what has happened. Is my father, Peter trying to tell me something from beyond? Or has my uncle Charles somehow come into my dream?

Then it dawns on me I have the same name as my uncle. Why would my parents call me after my uncle if the brothers weren't talking?

Margaret is next to me on the sun lounge on our deck reading the Sunday paper. I turn to her saying, "I think my father, or maybe my uncle, has been telling me this story. This is what the dream is all about."

"Charlie, you know I'm a scientist and shouldn't believe in mysterious things like dreams. Still, there must be something in this otherwise how else would you have found out all this about your family?"

"Science can't explain everything, Margaret. For me, I am comforted by the fact I now know why and who I have been dreaming about. Whether it's Peter, my dad, or Charles, my uncle, it feels good to know I have more family. I feel complete for the first time in my life."

"Complete? What do you mean?"

"I'm not sure to tell the truth. With my father being quiet about his past I have always wondered what the mystery was all about. There was something missing and there were times I just wanted to know. There is something bothering me though. My mother told me that the brothers didn't talk. So, why am I named after my uncle?"

"I had wondered that too, but I didn't want to bring it up. I thought you would have already known the reason. Anyway, was it your dad or your uncle on the road that night?"

"I think it's my uncle. My dad lived here in Sydney and he had no reason to be in New York. Charles was married to Patricia, who was a Rothburgh. Can you imagine their worth once they were married? Both families were hideously rich."

"Sounds like money didn't help him much. I assume he lived a miserable life once his wife and son died."

Charlie ponders what Margaret has said. It seems in his uncle's case money didn't buy happiness. The mystery remains as to why I'm named Charlie.

∼

After dinner we are relaxed in front of the TV. I'm bored and am flicking stations when a documentary catches my eye. Settling on the ABC, we begin watching the documentary that is set in New York.

"Oh my, this is about the Rothburgh family." Margaret stops reading and watches with me.

"I know, what a coincidence."

Pressing the information button on the remote, the title comes up – *The Tragedy of the Rothburgh Curse.*

We both settle in and watch in awe how there actually was a curse on this family. Patricia had two older brothers who were killed in WWII, her younger sister was born with a disability and died before her twentieth birthday and their grandfather died at thirty from a heart attack.

"… and it seems the Rothburgh curse extended itself into the families that married into the Rothburgh family. Patricia's husband, Charles Zellonica caused a tragic accident…"

"They're talking about my uncle. He's to blame for his wife's and child's deaths."

"You knew there were tragic circumstances in the dream and this documentary proves you were right."

"Margaret, as fascinating it is that I have rich family members in New York, I'm grateful that my father moved away. We could have been a part of that curse."

She nods at me with a contemplative look. We continue watching this fascinating documentary.

The next few weeks fly as I help Margaret collate all the findings from my research along with what we gathered from the documentary. I had contacted the documentary makers and they gave me more information about my Uncle Charles. As much as he started his business with family money, it was his expertise with maths that made him even more successful. He was a genius. Unfortunately, this, the sleepwalking and the death of his family had driven him to madness. He spent his last twenty years in a mental institution. I felt despondent when I read this. The Rothburghs family curse had certainly taken him.

I was also able to find out the reason for my name. Every male child born in the Zellonica family was named Charles. It was tradition and dated back to the 1500s. I guess my father broke slightly with tradition by naming me Charlie. My birth certificate shows Charlie and I have been known by this diminutive of Charles all my life.

James walks into my office as I'm packing up to go home. He has his winter coat draped over his arm, his scarf loosely hanging from his neck. We're both about to head out into the early spring evening, the chill of winter is on its way out.

"Only two months to go until the Flauncey. We have a lot to organise."

"I know, James. With the seven-point management plan for sleepwalkers finally confirmed and working, we will be able to concentrate on finalising some type of cure."

"You and your team have certainly worked hard enough, Margaret. I know you're close." His hand reaches for my arm and I flinch.

I give him a weak smile as we both walk out of my office. I stay further away from him than I need to. The night air seeps through me the minute we walk outside. I'm not as confident as he is about this medal but I like his enthusiasm. Although, I need to work out how to handle his unwanted attention.

Thinking about Charlie's episodes as I drive home, I realise he hasn't spoken of any since watching the documentary.

Sitting at the dinner table, we have been chatting about incidental things when I ask Charlie about his episodes.

"I was wondering when you would notice I haven't had one for a while. I've been sleeping well since watching that documentary."

"That was months ago. Do you think this is a breakthrough?"

"I certainly hope so. I had a few too many all at once, it was exhausting."

"Oh, I agree. You had two a week there at one stage."

"Yes, and I disturbed your sleep too. There were times when you woke up because I had knocked into something or broken things. How did I not cut myself after breaking those glasses?"

"You were lucky, I guess. Anyway, it looks like the sleep routine you have established as part of the seven-part management plan is doing some good."

"I think you're right. But I also think the fact I have learned about my extended family has something to do with it. Remember when I told you I felt more complete? Well, I'm more relaxed and this is helping me have better sleep."

We continue talking and I'm pleased to hear he is more relaxed. Mind you, this I have noticed because he is not on edge any longer. I feel relief knowing my research has had some worth. Knowing many other sufferers will benefit too gives a satisfaction that is gratifying.

My team and I are in the boardroom going through all the papers and checking they are all documented in the right folders. As I supervise the work, I hear their chatter about what they have done over the weekend. Most of my team are in their early thirties. Bright, young minds, the eight of them have poured many hours into this research without complaint. And it will benefit them in their future careers.

Once we have completed all the files, I turn the conversation to the Flauncey Medal. "Right, we need to concentrate on what we will present to the board in early November. I know the seven-part management system is a start, but a cure is our aim."

We continue with this topic for the rest of the afternoon. One of my team adds that he thinks cognitive therapy will help sufferers and we might need to add this to the treatment. As far as a cure, he is sceptical we will find one before the ceremony. The others nod.

"A cure is further away, I agree. What I would like to see is a formula or some form of trajectory to a cure. We are seventy percent there and if we are able to give them a timeline this may help us over the line."

The discussion stays on this topic until late into the evening.

"Ok, I think we've done enough for one day. Thank you all for staying late."

Everyone begins packing up and we head to our cars. They wish me a good night and I know some of them will kick on somewhere, probably the local pub. I too am feeling a buzz from what we have achieved so far. My dream of helping sleepwalkers with severe conditions is achievable, I am beginning to feel it.

Driving home I crank the music loud. The strains of Vivaldi's *Four Seasons* fill my ears as I tap along.

James is there to greet Charlie and I as we walk into the grand ballroom at the Sheraton on the Park. He compliments me on my red off-the-shoulder gown and Charlie for looking dapper. I notice Charlie flinching slightly but admire him for not reacting more. Ursula had again helped me with my hair and make-up, outdoing herself this time. She had told me she had read up on this award and knew it was a prestigious one. "You will outshine everyone, I will make sure of it," she had said.

"Charlie, even you have brushed up well tonight," continues James.

"Thanks, but I didn't want to outshine this gorgeous woman." He says this waving his hand up and down in front of me. He is making an effort to lighten the situation.

"With this gown I'll outshine everyone," I joke laughing nervously trying to lighten my own mood. I have never been so wired up. When James received notification that we were in the top three for the medal, he was not able to contain his excitement. It was infectious and myself and my team have been carrying this feeling for two weeks.

I'm overwhelmed as we head to our table. This room holds over five hundred and our table is towards the front. Each table is laden with long clear vases of white lilies, roses and orchids. The magnificent orchids swoop down towards the white tablecloths. Ten people will sit around each table and enjoy a three-course meal on the fine china over-sized plates. There is more cutlery, glasses and crockery on these tables than we have in our kitchen cupboards.

Charlie assists me to sit making sure my gown isn't caught under the chair legs. We greet the others already seated and we all mention how we are all a bundle of nerves. Somehow this calms me a little, knowing I'm not the only one feeling this way.

The MC walks onstage and I smile as I recognise him. Anthony Demuri welcomes everyone as he glances down to where I'm sitting. His smile beams and I become flustered. Picking up the champagne flute and drink it all. I hadn't even noticed it had been filled.

Anthony introduces dignitaries. There is loud applause that is doubled when he announces the nominees and asks us to stand. "Let the festivities begin," he says over the applause.

Taking our seats again, the food begins to be served. Whether it is my nerves or the fact I am overwhelmed, I pick at what is in front of me. All this gourmet food and I'm not interested. Beginning to wish this night was over, I hold onto Charlie's leg.

"Are you ok, darling?"

"Feeling like this is all too much. I want it over."

"It's normal to feel this way when your life's work is being acknowledged. Take a few deep breaths and try to enjoy the evening."

His reassuring words calm me a little, so I focus on the conversation at our table when there is a tap on my shoulder. I turn to see Anthony.

"I wanted to give you my congratulations. Whether your team wins or not tonight, to me you are already a winner."

"Why thank you, Anthony. That's very nice of you. And it's lovely to see you again. How is everything with you?"

"Well, remember I mentioned I wanted to go into television? Well, I've been offered a position with Channel 7 as their health reporter. I'll be doing spots for the news and other shows they are planning."

"Anthony, that's wonderful. I'm happy for you. Congratulations, I'm sure you will do well."

"Thanks, I wanted to tell you before you saw me on TV. Now, I had better go, the speeches will be starting soon. And then the big announcement will happen."

"It was nice of you to come over to speak to me. Good luck with everything."

When I turn back to the table everyone starts asking me what Anthony had wanted. When I tell them, they are happy to hear he is succeeding in his career. I guess he's a winner too.

I begin to feel weary as the speeches drone on. It's after ten and there has been no mention of the reason we are here tonight, who is winning the medal? The money that comes with winning this medal will assist the university in funding more research and we are all keen to find out who the winner will be. I'm becoming annoyed and want them to get on with it.

Charlie places his hand on my left leg asking me to calm down. I hadn't realised my leg was twitching, a sure sign that I am nervous.

"It won't be long now, this should be the last speaker."

"I hope so." I say this while taking a gulp of my wine.

As it turns out, Charlie was right. Anthony comes back on stage and announces what we've all waited to hear, that the announcement is happening. He has the envelope in his hand and asks the board of the Flauncey Medal to join him onstage.

There had been a band playing most of the night. I had hardly noticed them due to my nerves, but now they play louder as Anthony holds up the envelope and opens it.

We all stand up as our university is named. There are whoops and hollers, wolf-whistles and tears as we hug each other. Myself and my team members head to the stage, patting each other on the back.

I am handed the medal that is encased in a navy-blue velvet case and hold it up for everyone to see. Then I turn it towards me, smile and hand it to my team members.

Clearing my throat, I begin my speech. The rest of the night is a blur of congratulations, dancing and feeling elated that we won. James had come over and given me a huge hug and kisses. Charlie had jumped up and placed his arm over my shoulders the minute James stepped back. He was marking me as his and giving James a message. Taking my hand, Charlie led me to the dance floor and we spent most of the night dancing. I remember everyone giving their congratulations to myself and the team again when it was time to leave. This time James shook my hand. By the time we were in the limousine going home, it was two in the morning and we're both in burnout mode.

∽

The next morning my head is as heavy as a rock. Charlie walks in with a coffee announcing he had made it short and strong.

"Thanks," I say taking it and drinking it in one go.

"Have you come down to earth yet?"

"No, and I don't want to. I'm going to enjoy this for some time."

"I don't blame you. And I want to thank you because I haven't had an episode in six months. That's somewhat of a record."

"You had a lot to do with it, Charlie. Without the discipline you have given to the management of your condition, it would not have happened."

"Either way, the combination of your hard work and my determination has hopefully cured me of sleepwalking."

"I hope you're right. My team and I still have work to do in finding a cure but the funds from the medal will go a long way in making it happen."

"Yes, congratulations again," he says bending to kiss my cheek, "I'm going to throw the white shoe out. It was Patricia's shoe not my late wife Alexandra's, so I don't see a reason to keep it. Hopefully this is closure for me, and I look forward to never sleepwalking again."

I kiss him gently on his cheek. He has gone through some emotional turmoil and I do hope it is the end of this drama. I will make it my mission to find a cure for people who suffer from chronic sleepwalking.

THE END

WOMEN ABOUT WOMEN

How this group started…

"Let's start a writing group for women. Women writing about women."

It was Joanna who suggested this with Conchita quickly agreeing. And so began **Women About Women** with Joanna and Conchita as co-creators of the group. Soon Maria P, Adelaide and Marjorie joined. Then there were more interested writers and this was when Maria, Irina and Maree came on board.

These eight authors along with two editors, Rachel and Teresa, formed **Women About Women** and have contributed their passion, ideas, creativity, experience, drive… and of course, their stories. Each story has its own genre and style, with each being as different as the authors who wrote them.

In between meetings, each author was weaving her story that would flourish in a compendium of stories where women were the protagonists, sometimes quite the hero, sometimes searching for the truth, or simply making casseroles or being funny.

The result is, *Weaving Words*, a collaboration of ten passionate women and their stories.

ACKNOWLEDGMENTS

A project of this magnitude takes many to help it come to fruition. *Weaving Words* would not have been possible without the help of other professionals. We would like to acknowledge the support of these people who helped us to publish this anthology.

Thank you to Rachel New, our lovely editor. Rachel read each story and polished them where required. Also, to Teresa Goudie for helping with the editing when we started and for the Style Guide she prepared.

Teresa had this to say regarding the group dynamic – "I think that the way you all read each other's stories, and help one another through your feedback, is such a wonderful way to learn and share. It's refreshing to see such support and camaraderie!"

To Maria Issaris for her wonderful production of our audio book. Along with the narrators she has given us another version of the anthology that readers can enjoy listening to.

We are all very grateful to writer Cass Moriarty who kindly read our stories and delivered a beautiful foreword. Her words towards our writing made us believe in ourselves and encouraged us to carry on with this amazing creative activity.

Thank you as well to Liam Prendergast, a graphic designer who worked with us to design the cover of our book. Liam interpreted the ideas of the eight authors very well, we all love the cover of *Weaving Words*.

We would also like to acknowledge the work by Laura Hugill, laura. hugill@gmail.com for her work on the cover design concepts.

To the wonderful women who make up the **Women About Women** group, the cohesive way we all worked together has produced a series of short stories that we can all be proud of.

www.ingramcontent.com/pod-product-compliance
Lightning Source LLC
Chambersburg PA
CBHW070251010526
44107CB00056B/2423